958.104   Herda, D. J.   37134
HER
✓   The Afghan Rebels

$12.90

DATE			

© THE BAKER & TAYLOR CO.

THE AFGHAN REBELS

Maps by Joe Le Monnier

Photographs courtesy of:
Photo Researchers: pp. 8 (Ian Graham), 17, 78
(Eugene Gordon), 35 (P. J. Hollaway), 41 (Paolo
Koch), 58 (Thomas Baird); Magnum: pp. 10, 21,
45, (Marc Riboud), 14, 39, 42, 51, 73, 117, 118
(Steve McCurry), 47, 60, 68, (Ed Grazda); UPI/
Bettmann Newsphotos: pp. 24, 28, 32, 110, 112;
AP/Wide World: p. 100.

Library of Congress Cataloging-in-Publication Data

Herda, D. J., 1948–
The Afghan Rebels : the war in Afghanistan / D.J. Herda.
p.   cm.
Includes bibliographical references.
Summary: An account of the ten-year war in Afghanistan from its
political origins to the Soviet withdrawal in 1989.
ISBN   0-531-10897-X
1. Afghanistan—History—Soviet occupation, 1979–1989—Juvenile
literature.   I. Title.
DS371.2.H47   1990
958.104'5—dc20   89-22603   CIP   AC

CONTENTS

THE AFGHAN REBELS

INTRODUCTION

In April 1978, a bloody coup launched against the ruling royal lineage of Afghanistan brought to power a radical, pro-Soviet political party and set the stage for war. It was the beginning of Afghanistan's "glorious revolution," according to the new Marxist regime, and the end of an era for Afghanistan.

It also marked a change for the Soviet Union, Afghanistan's neighbor to the north. The Soviets claimed that the coup posed a threat to them, and thus they had a right to invade Afghanistan. But as the Afghan revolution grew into a war that ultimately evolved into one of the most violent and deadly conflicts in modern history, the Soviets were forced to reevaluate their long-standing policies of armed intervention in Europe, South America, Africa, Asia, and the Caribbean.

The Afghan Rebels is the story of Afghanistan from its occupation by Soviet troops in 1979 through their departure ten years later. But it is more than that. It is also the tale of one nation's valiant fight against the unlawful invasion by another. It is the history of a rugged and starkly beautiful land from its beginnings to

*Afghanistan is a rugged and
starkly beautiful land.*

its fledgling life as a developing nation-state. It is the saga of the Afghan people and their struggle for freedom and a look at the events that have shaped Afghan history and the politics, religion, and economics of a nation.

* * *

While writing a book about Afghanistan more than a decade ago, this author was fortunate to come to know the people and their land intimately. I was putting the final touches on the book in 1979 when I picked up the morning paper and read the shocking news. "Soviets Invade Afghanistan," the headlines screamed. I scanned those early stories in horror, trying to find some meaning in the events. Why Afghanistan? Why the Soviet Union? What was the meaning of it? Where would it end?

During the years between then and now, I've met and befriended many loyal Afghans—people dedicated to overthrowing a despotic government and expelling the foreign invaders. Some of these Afghans have been shuttling regularly between the United States and their native land or neighboring Pakistan for more than a decade. Many belong to underground movements dedicated to supporting the rebels fighting in Afghanistan. Nearly all have friends, relatives, and neighbors still living in their homeland.

In my travels through Asia during the 1980s, I was able to develop many contacts, via the underground, with Afghan rebels and their families, all of whom were fighting for their freedom—and sometimes their lives. As I met and talked with these brave people, I slowly began finding answers to the questions I had asked in the early days of the Soviet occupation, and I became intent upon telling their stories to the world.

Many of the personal accounts in this book are based upon firsthand information relayed to me by members of the various Afghan resistance movements, including the Afghan Resistance League, the *Hezb-i Islami*, the *Sazman-e Jawanan-e Musalman*, and other organizations whose members are bound together for the common goal of securing a free Afghanistan for Afghans. Because the fight for Afghanistan still rages at the time of this writing, we have chosen to alter some names, dates, and locations to protect the patriots involved and to reduce the possibility of Soviet-backed government reprisals against the rebels, their families, and their friends still living and fighting inside Afghanistan. All incidents are based upon fact.

Although we have made every attempt to retain the integrity of the many different languages and dialects used throughout Afghanistan and the surrounding region by relying on the most literal and accurate translations available, some minor phonetic variations may exist.

D. J. Herda
Middleton, Wisconsin
Summer 1989

CHAPTER ONE
THE BEGINNING

In Afghanistan, they're called *mujahedin* (moo-jah-hah-dean), which means warriors of Islam, holy warriors, protectors of the faith, resistance fighters, resisters, or rebels. Many consider them to be the true loyalists of Afghanistan, those who have remained faithful to their political, social, and religious beliefs in the face of foreign aggression. They are people fighting for the integrity of their country.

Mujahedin don't switch name tags or allegiances the way some people change socks. They don't temper their beliefs because someone tells them to do so. They don't alter their way of life—a life that has existed relatively unchanged for more than 2,000 years—even when threatened by danger or death.

Despite savage warring, the *mujahedin,* like most Afghans, are a peace-loving people. They are friendly and warm toward other Afghans, helpful and respectful toward outsiders. Yet, they have been at war with one group of people or another for what seems like most of their existence on earth.

The story of the rugged, mountainous nation of Afghanistan goes back much farther than a hundred or

A member of the mujahedin

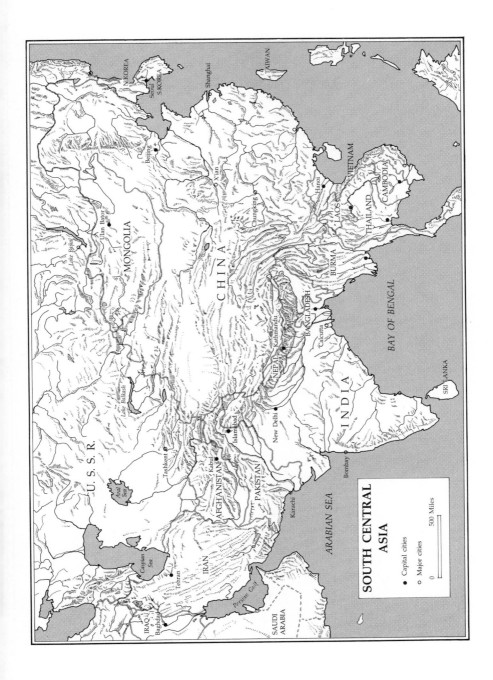

SOUTH CENTRAL
ASIA

● Capital cities

○ Major cities

0   500 Miles

two hundred or even five hundred years. It's a story that started before humans existed. It's the story of the land.

Afghanistan lies at the very crossroads of Asia, bordered on the west by Iran, on the north by the Soviet Union, on the northeast by China, and on the east and south by Pakistan. Most of the country is mountainous, cut in two by an extension of the Himalayas called the Hindu Kush, the most spectacular of all the towering Afghan ranges, reaching a height of 25,236 feet (7,690 m) and stretching for more than 500 miles (800 km). The Afghan word *kush* means death and was probably given to the mountains because of the treacherous passes between the peaks. Of Afghanistan's total land area, nearly 50 percent lies at 6,560 feet (2,000 m) above sea level.

Afghanistan's mountainous regions are young and rugged, with sharp peaks, deep valleys, and many nearly impenetrable barriers. The fertile valleys and plains nestled between the numerous ranges have always been home to most of the area's population.

The land of Afghanistan is mostly dry. Numerous rivers crisscross the country, many of which, however, are little more than summer runoffs from the permanently snow-covered peaks feeding the principal rivers, the Indus and the Amu Darya. They are mostly unnavigable, swollen and raging in the spring and low and sluggish by the end of summer. But the Afghans have found a way to use them, by way of a complex system of underground tunnels, to irrigate their fields. Agriculture is the backbone of the Afghan economy, with approximately 10 percent of the land in corn, barley, rice, and fruit cultivation. The rest of the land is mostly nonarable. Besides agriculture, Afghans raise sheep for their skins, wool, and meat.

*Fertile valleys and rich farmlands are surrounded
by the forbidding peaks of the Hindu Kush.*

Despite the inhospitable setting that tends to isolate it from the rest of the world, Afghanistan has fallen prey to many conquerors through the ages. The country sits astride the famed Khyber Pass, the greatest single land route from the west through the Hindu Kush to Pakistan and the important trading centers of India.

There are other passageways between east and west, known mostly to the nomadic shepherds who move from one traditional grazing ground to another with the changing of the seasons. Each fall, tens of thousands of nomads, like the ghosts of their ancestors, follow ancient passes to the grazing grounds from Afghanistan to what is known today as Pakistan. When spring arrives, they return to Afghanistan.

But if you ask these shepherds if they are Afghan or Pakistani, they stare blankly at you. In their minds, they are neither Afghan nor Pakistani, but free. They have no state except wherever the grass grows.

Although a large number of Afghans don't consider themselves members of a particular political state, nearly all belong to one of the many tribal or ethnic groups that make up Afghanistan.

Most Afghans (about 6.5 million of the total population of 15 million) belong to an ethnic group known as Pashtun. The majority of Pashtuns speak Pashtu, although many Pashtuns living in the capital city of Kabul speak the Persian dialect of Dari. Both languages—Pashtu and Dari—belong to the Iranian branch of the Indo-European language family. About 3.5 million Afghans are Tajiks, who generally live in the west around the city of Herat, as well as in the north, in the rugged Pamir mountain area of the Wakhan Corridor. They speak various Iranian dialects. The Farsiwans, or Persians, speak Dari and live primarily in

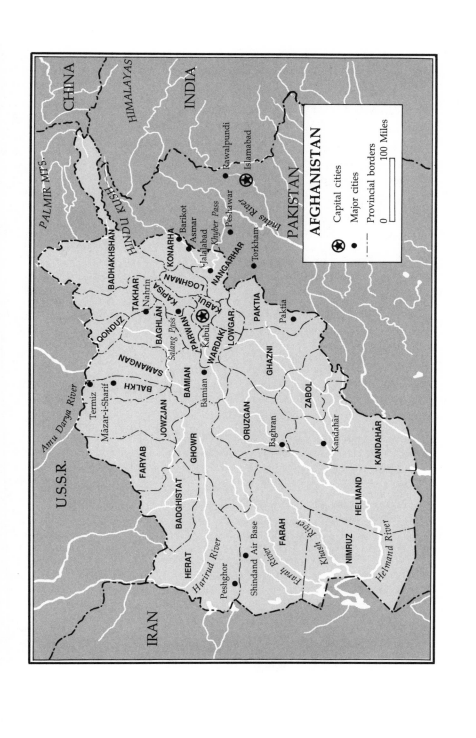

AFGHANISTAN

⊛ Capital cities

• Major cities

—·—·— Provincial borders

0 — 100 Miles

CHINA

HIMALAYAS

PALMIR MTS.

HINDU KUSH

INDIA

Rawalpundi

Islamabad

PAKISTAN

Indus River

Barikot

Asmar

Khyber Pass

Peshawar

Jalalabad

Torkham

BADHAKHSHAN

KONARHA

NANGARHAR

LOGHMAN

TAKHAR

Nahrin

KAPISA

QONDUZ

BAGHLAN

Salang Pass

PARWAN

KABUL

Kabul

LOWGAR

PAKTIA

Paktia

SAMANGAN

WARDAKI

BALKH

BAMIAN

GHAZNI

Termiz

Mazar-i-Sharif

Bamian

ZABOL

JOWZJAN

ORUZGAN

Baghran

Kandahar

Amu Darya River

FARYAB

GHOWR

KANDAHAR

U.S.S.R.

BADGHISTAT

HELMAND

HERAT

Harirud River

Peshghor

Shindand Air Base

FARAH

NIMRUZ

Farah River

Khash River

Helmand River

IRAN

western Afghanistan near the Iranian border. The Hazaras speak a dialect of Dari and live primarily in central Afghanistan. The Uzbeks (about a million of them) speak Uzbek, a Turkish dialect, and live in north-central Afghanistan, while a small population of Turkmen are scattered throughout the northernmost portion of Afghanistan along the Soviet border. Numerous smaller ethnic groups complete the complicated Afghan society.

Afghanistan's great ethnic diversity is both a major strength and one of its greatest weaknesses. Although so many diverse cultures make the people difficult to conquer, they also make them difficult to unite. Marco Polo, writing about the Afghans' nomadic life-style more than seven centuries ago, said, "The mountains afford pasture for an innumerable quantity of sheep, which ramble about in flocks while the herders follow." More than six hundred years later, Karl Marx wrote after visiting the area that Afghanistan was not a country at all but more a poetic term for numerous tribes and states of mind.

No matter what they're called, the Afghans, pushing their herds of sheep, horses, camels, and cattle before them, have traveled these lands throughout history from pasture to pasture, interrupted periodically by such conquerors as Darius I (circa 500 B.C.), who sought to reunite the ancient Persian kingdoms; Alexander the Great (356–323 B.C.), who admired the Afghans' fast, proud horses; Genghis Khan (circa 1220 A.D.), who sought to conquer the world; Tamerlane (circa 1400 A.D.) on his march to conquer China; and countless Arab invaders from the seventh century A.D. Each came with great armies of warriors, seized control of the land, and tormented the Afghans for a

*The nomadic Afghan tribes live today as
their ancestors lived hundreds of years ago.*

time before finally moving on to other more pressing goals—or simply passing into the obscure pages of history. Then the Afghans resumed their shuttling back and forth from green to green, exhibiting little more than a mild annoyance at the disruption to their lives.

In the nineteenth century, more serious challenges to the Afghans came from colonial India. The British there sought to fortify Afghanistan in an attempt to protect the British Empire from Russian expansion. The two British-Afghan wars (1839–1842 and 1878–1879) ended in an agreement in 1907 turning control of Afghanistan's foreign affairs over to the British. But in 1919, Afghanistan was given complete independence.

As the various conquerors marched through the valleys of Afghanistan along the path that traders called the "silk route" to the East, they brought with them diverse cultures and religions. The Hellenic culture touched the Afghan peoples, as did Buddhism, which arrived from India but was replaced by Islam in the seventh century A.D. The Hindus and Sikhs, originally traders from India, as well as the Jews, also left their marks on Afghan society, although today the country is nearly all Muslim.

Despite their common Islamic beliefs, however, the Afghans are anything but unified. In fact, they're split into many different Islamic tribes or sects, including the Sunni, Shiite, Ismaili, and Sufi.

These diverse and frequently warring peoples were first united into a single nation-state in 1747 by Ahmad Shah Durrani. His descendants ruled the nation with only minor interruptions for more than two centuries until 1978, continuing even after the monarchy was abolished in 1973 and a republic was established by Prince Sardar Mohammad Daoud Khan, a senior member of the royal family.

On April 27, 1978, elements of the Marxist-oriented Afghan armed forces succeeded in a coup d'etat that toppled the regime of President Daoud. Just days later, the Revolutionary Council of the Democratic Republic of Afghanistan (DRA) gained power. Nur Mohammad Taraki of the People's Democratic Party of Afghanistan (PDPA), a Marxist party whose following was largely limited to an educated minority in urban areas of the country, was appointed chairman of the revolutionary government and prime minister. Taraki quickly attempted to bring seventeenth-century Afghanistan into the twentieth century by upgrading the status of Afghan women, instituting new laws regulating marriage, abolishing usury, developing both state and private sectors of the economy, and beginning various programs of land reform.

Although Taraki's programs were basically sound, they came too fast to suit most traditional Afghans. Also, many Afghans were alarmed by Taraki's repressive actions and the imprisonment and even execution of members of the political opposition. By late 1978, numerous insurrections had begun in various parts of the country. The PDPA was further weakened by bitter infighting. The situation worsened in 1979 when armed opposition to the Taraki regime spread to nearly every region of the country. Mutinies within the Afghan army were common. When Taraki attempted to remove Hafizullah Amin, an ambitious and astute party leader, from power, Amin turned the tables and had Taraki arrested after a wild shootout at the presidential palace in the capital city of Kabul. By October, Taraki was dead, presumably murdered in prison by a group of Amin's agents.

As the new head of state, Amin sought to preserve his country's independence and keep it free of Soviet

Amin addresses the United Nations in June 1978

influence. Despite several failed social and military programs, he issued a statement over Radio Afghanistan saying that Afghanistan was capable of handling its own affairs. It was a warning to the Soviets to maintain a hands-off policy toward Afghanistan. He went on to state that Afghanistan was an independent, nonaligned nation, meaning it was not to be considered by Moscow to be an extension of the Soviet-dominated Eastern Bloc. Although Soviet leaders Leonid Brezhnev and Alexei Kosygin sent congratulations to Amin on his election to the position of PDPA secretary general, they were already beginning to worry about Amin's anti-Soviet stance.

From the very start, Amin proved himself to be an able and effective leader. One of his earliest official acts was to appoint a fifty-seven-member constitutional committee to revise or rewrite the Afghan constitution. Amin established a special revolutionary court to review the cases of political prisoners held in Afghan jails since April 1978. He renamed the secret police the Workers' Intelligence Institute (KAM) and promised that it would operate within the framework of Afghan law.

In the meantime, tensions with neighboring Pakistan were increasing daily because the *mujahedin* guerrillas, who were opposed to Amin's secular form of government and the manner in which he had grabbed power, were using camps in Pakistan as bases from which to launch attacks into Afghanistan. By autumn of 1979, nearly 230,000 Afghan refugees and guerrillas resided in Pakistan, with as many as 9,000 crossing the border weekly. Amin believed that a strong alliance with Pakistan might stop the Soviet Union from intervening in Afghan political affairs—one of his greatest fears—so he took initiatives to establish closer relations. But the Soviets had their own plans.

In late November, Soviet First Deputy Minister of the Interior, Lieutenant-General Viktor S. Paputin, arrived in Kabul on a fact-finding tour. Four days after his departure for the Soviet Union on December 13, there was a shooting at the House of the People, and Amin was reportedly wounded in the leg. Amin believed the assassination attempt was arranged by Paputin under orders from Moscow, and on December 19, he fled with a contingent of loyal Afghan troops to the Darulaman Palace on the southern edge of Kabul.

The Soviets saw a chance to act. While Amin was gone, they sent their elite 105th Guards Airborne Division from Fergana in the Tadzhik Soviet Socialist Republic to Bagram Airbase near Kabul. By early December, Soviet paratroop strength in Kabul numbered 2,500 men. On December 20, a Soviet armored unit secured the vital Salang Tunnel, the major overland route from the Soviet Union into Afghanistan.

On Christmas Eve of 1979, at 11 P.M., the Soviet airlift began. Troops and materials arrived primarily at Kabul International Airport, as well as at the nearby air bases of Bagram, Shindand, and Kandahār. One witness recalls, "The planes started landing at night. You couldn't see anything, it was so dark. You could only hear the constant roar of their engines overhead. For two days and three nights, the planes kept landing without a break." By December 27, nearly 5,000 Soviet troops occupied Kabul. That's when the Soviet Union switched into high gear.

The Soviets secured the center of Kabul by evening, although resistance continued at the Darulaman Palace until the early hours of December 28. Shortly thereafter, an official announcement was made: Amin had been sentenced to death by a "Revolutionary Tribunal." Most independent sources, however, believe that Amin, true to Afghan tradition, died fighting the foreign invaders.

On December 27 at 8:45 P.M., a Soviet radio transmitter in Termez broadcast a statement by Babrak Karmal, a gifted orator and long-time participant in Afghan politics, denouncing the "intolerable violence and torture by the bloody apparatus of Amin" and announcing a "national *jihad* [holy war] of the Afghan people for true democratic justice, for respect for the holy Islamic religion . . . and for implementation of the aims of the glorious . . . revolution." Further broadcasts transmitted from Kabul named Karmal president of the new revolutionary council, prime minister of the government, and secretary general of the PDPA.

Early the next morning, Soviet-controlled Radio Afghanistan broadcast a request for "political, moral, and economic assistance, including military aid" from the Soviet Union, in what surely was a thinly veiled Soviet ploy to justify the USSR's presence in Afghanistan.

Although the Karmal regime indicated that the Soviets' presence would be shortlived, few Western observers believed it. It appeared likely that the Soviets planned to stay in Afghanistan for at least ten to fifteen years, for the same reason they came to Afghanistan— to install and preserve a regime that was friendly to them. The Soviets' long-term goals for Afghanistan seemed obvious, as evidenced by their sending Afghan children, particularly war orphans, to the Soviet Union to be educated in the doctrines of Marx and the Soviet communist party. The Soviets assumed that, upon returning to their native Afghanistan ten to fifteen years later, these indoctrinated young people would take charge of the by-then well-established Marxist Afghan government.

The Soviets made a commitment to promote literacy, health, and a higher standard of living among the Afghans. Living standards in independent Afghanistan were among the poorest in the world. Perhaps once the Soviets had demonstrated to the Afghans the benefits of prosperity coupled with military might and a Soviet style of education, the new generation of Afghans would fall into line with Soviet policy.

One month after the Soviet invasion, 40,000 Soviet troops had been moved into position in Afghanistan. Nearly 10,000 of them proved to be of little value and were soon returned to Russia. These were mostly heavy artillery units and tank battalions that were replaced by infantry units, helicopter gunships—helicopters fitted with machine guns and rockets—and light ground forces better suited to the mountainous terrain and hit-and-run tactics employed by the Afghan rebels. By the end of 1980, the Soviets had boosted their troop strength to nearly 85,000 men.

Babrak Karmal

CHAPTER TWO
THE MOUNTING STAKES

In the earliest days of their occupation, the Soviets limited their combat strength to the number of troops necessary to gain and hold control of Afghanistan's major roads, towns, and cities. One of the Soviet Union's greatest obstacles proved to be the Afghan army. These army troops, about 25,000 soldiers under the leadership of Soviet-installed Afghan president Babrak Karmal, often chose to side with the rebels. Eventually, Soviet forces ended up turning heavy weapons against the very troops whose fledgling Marxist government they had been sent to support.

The Soviets also suffered large numbers of casualties in their attempts to subdue several major Afghan army mutinies, including one by the 8th Infantry Division in January 1980 and another even more bloody mutiny by the 14th Armored Division in July of the same year.

Meanwhile, worldwide anger over the Soviet invasion of Afghanistan was mounting. Bolstered by American President Jimmy Carter's announcement in a speech on January 4, 1980, that the United States would impose a grain embargo and halt the sale of high-technology equipment to the Russians in response to the invasion, representatives of five Afghan rebel groups met in Peshawar, Pakistan, in an attempt to form a united front against the Soviet-installed Kabul government. For perhaps the first time in history, diverse Afghan tribes were joining together to fight a common foe.

On January 7, 1980, the U.N. Security Council voted 13 to 2 in favor of a resolution condemning the Soviet Union for invading Afghanistan and demanding an immediate withdrawal of all troops. The resolution was defeated by Soviet and East German vetoes.

The U.N. resolution was eventually passed from the Security Council to the General Assembly, where on January 14, 1980, a resolution was adopted deploring the Soviet invasion and calling for "the immediate, unconditional, and total withdrawal of the foreign troops" in that country. The resolution, without mentioning the Soviet Union by name, was adopted by a vote of 104 to 18. Many of the Asian, African, and Latin American countries that normally sided with Moscow voted in favor of the resolution. In Canada, Prime Minister Joe Clark sent messages to Soviet President Leonid Brezhnev and Afghan President Babrak Karmal announcing that his country was cutting off all aid to Afghanistan until Soviet troops were withdrawn.

In the Middle East, Saudi Arabia announced that it would boycott the 1980 Olympic Games in Moscow in protest of the Soviet invasion. Although the North Atlantic Treaty Organization (NATO) discussed the possibility of an international boycott of the games in a meeting in Brussels on December 30, 1979, most nations—including the United States—were hesitant to approve such a move. President Carter did, later, decide to boycott the games.

In neighboring Pakistan, President Mohammad Zia ul-Haq in a public address on January 8, 1980, warned, "If the human community remains a silent spectator, then the small countries . . . will not be able to live on the face of the earth."

Despite mounting international pressure, the Soviets, convinced they could win a quick and decisive victory in Afghanistan, continued their assault, sending task forces to battle the *mujahedin* rebels in the Panjshir Valley in February, Jalalabad in March, and Herat in September of 1980. The Soviets began hurling heavy bombs and artillery at the *mujahedin* and their strongholds, including Herat, Kandahār, and Jalalabad, in 1981.

Many of the Soviets' earliest campaigns against the Afghan rebels were failures. Guerrilla strength in the Panjshir Valley threatened the major Soviet supply line from the capital city of Kabul to the northern Afghan city of Mazār-i-Sharif by way of Salang Tunnel (the scene of several Soviet assaults). A large but inexperienced Soviet motorized rifle battalion in the town of Paktia left the main road and was destroyed when its troops panicked and hid behind their vehicles until their ammunition ran out and they were killed. Such incidents quickly convinced the Soviets that they needed to employ smaller tactical units that could be moved more quickly and efficiently from one area of the country to another.

Pakistan's President Mohammad Zia ul-Haq (later killed in a plane crash)

The Soviets also encountered difficulties with several Turkestan Military District motorized rifle divisions that had been raised to combat strength by calling Afghan army reservists to active duty. The Central Asian soldiers who made up the units often fraternized with rebel forces, especially the Tajiks, with whom they had close ethnic ties. Eventually, the Soviets replaced the troops with Russian soldiers, on whose loyalties they could depend.

To hold the number of Soviet troops to a minimum and try to legitimize their presence in Afghanistan, the Soviet Union attempted to rebuild the Afghan army, which was quickly being depleted by desertions. First, they offered Afghan soldiers such inducements as pay raises and reenlistment bonuses. Then they enacted tougher conscription laws. But Afghan soldiers resisted orders to turn their weapons on their fellow Muslims and often resented taking orders from *farangi*, or foreigners.

During their nineteenth-century skirmishes with the Afghans, the colonial British used to claim that the Afghans' loyalties could be rented but never bought. Most Afghans remain loyal to themselves, their families, their country, and their government—in that order. An example of the strength of these loyalties occurred near the Pakistan border, where the Soviets had armed and trained 400 Afridi tribesmen to fight the *mujahedin*. When the Soviets brought the tribesmen into battle, the Afridis circled around, trapping and killing the Soviets in a crossfire with the rebels before slipping across the border into Pakistan.

In 1981, the rebels launched a war of terror against the Soviets and their puppet regime in the capital city of Kabul, sending several units into the city to attack PDPA and Soviet personnel. In January, a guerrilla

A street scene in the capital city of Kabul

group raided the large Soviet residential complex in Kabul, then attacked the headquarters of the Afghan secret police (KhAD, formerly known as KAM), which they destroyed. In April, three senior Afghan security officials were assassinated, including the commander of the defense militia and the second-ranking commander of Afghan military intelligence.

The Soviets responded by increasing their attacks in Logar Province, according to a broadcast over Radio Kabul, "to annihilate mercenaries, criminals, terrorists, and antirevolutionary elements, and to preserve the gains of the revolution." The Soviets' order of battle was usually fixed. They sent in Afghan militia first, followed by Afghan army units, with Soviet forces bringing up the rear. If the Afghans, sent in first to draw rebel fire, chose to desert (as they often did), the Soviets were in a good position to open fire on them.

By the end of 1981, Western intelligence sources reported that Warsaw Pact and Cuban military forces were being used by the Soviets in Afghanistan. There were also reports by guerrilla forces of Bulgarian troops and a Bulgarian military base in the northern city of Mazār-i-Sharif. Scattered reports of East German military personnel training Afghan security and police forces were also common.

Estimates of the number of Soviet helicopters and helicopter gunships in Afghanistan ranged from 500 to 650. Up to 250 of them were identified as Mi-24 Hind gunships. The Hind, with as many as 192 unguided rockets under its stub wings and machine guns or cannons in its turrets, can carry up to 12 soldiers with full battle gear. The Hind has also been used for search-and-destroy missions, close air support of ground troops, assaults (often in tandem with jet fighter support), and armed reconnaissance missions against Afghan rebel strongholds.

By 1982, the Soviets had developed a military procedure for using heavy air offensives to stun and disorganize rebel forces. The Soviets most often used Hind helicopters in a circular pattern to engage guerrillas directly, attacking in a dive from 1,000 meters with 57-mm rockets and high-explosive 250-kilogram bombs.

Later in the war, the tactics changed so that the helicopters (either Hinds or Mi-8 Hips) would go in as scouts, running from 8,000 meters away, rising to 100 meters and drawing fire from the ground, then moving out of danger while other more deadly aircraft—often MiG jet fighters—popped up from behind a ridge and attacked the *mujahedin* who had opened fire.

Although the Soviets insisted that their use of chemical weapons in Afghanistan was strictly defensive, the U. S. State Department received reports of forty-seven separate unprovoked chemical attacks between 1979 and mid-1981, resulting in the deaths of more than 3,000 people. These reports came from Afghan army deserters, Afghan rebels, journalists, and physicians. One report came from an Afghan army defector who gave the *Far Eastern Economic Review* details of Soviet-supplied chemical and biological agents used by Afghan army units. Other reports by foreign journalists suggested that the Soviets had dropped chemicals from helicopter units to drive guerrillas from caves or other hiding places and then attacked them with conventional weapons.

The Afghanistan invasion provided the Soviet Union with an opportunity to introduce and test several new weapons that hadn't previously been seen outside the USSR. One weapon specifically created for use in Afghanistan was the PMF-1 "butterfly" mine, with a "wing" that made it look like a butterfly or a sycamore seed. The mine spun slowly to the ground when dropped from the air. Small, constructed of green or brown (camouflaged) plastic, and powerful enough to blow off a foot or a hand, the mines were designed to blend in with the terrain and to maim rather than to kill. A maimed *mujahed,* the Soviets reasoned, took two or more men out of the war—the injured soldier and one or more others required to assist him.

Spread by Mi-8 Hip helicopters or large-caliber artillery, butterfly mines enabled the Soviets to sow a minefield quickly. A single Hip was capable of laying 144 mines in a solitary pass. Once released, the mines were scattered by airflow. The Soviets used the mines even though they had been banned by the Geneva Convention, which specifically forbids combatants to use mines that can't be detected by normal means and that have unlimited life spans. There's little doubt that butterfly mines can last a decade and are a threat both to Afghan children and to livestock.

Four other weapons introduced by the Soviets in Afghanistan included the 81-mm mortar, the AGS-17 automatic grenade launcher, the AK-74 high-velocity assault rifle, and the RPG-16 antitank weapon, capable of both rapid and continuous fire and of launching shells in a high trajectory, something that proved useful in the mountainous terrain of Afghanistan. The AGS-17 automatic grenade launcher could be mounted on a vehicle or used from a helicopter. Fired by two persons, it launches 30-mm grenades from a drum containing thirty rounds.

This boy lost his legs
when he encountered
a Soviet mine.

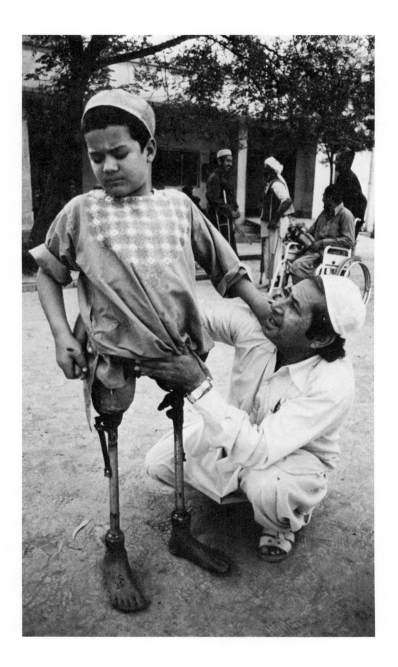

The AK-74 high-velocity assault rifle, a 5.45-mm caliber weapon equipped with an image-intensifying sight, resembles the standard AK-47 rifle but uses hollow-core bullets that are extremely damaging to human targets. The RPG-16 antitank weapon replaced the RPG-7 and represented an improvement both in range and accuracy.

During their first two years of occupation, the Soviets concentrated their efforts on gaining control of such major cities as Kandahār, Herat, and Kabul, thereby controlling the nerve centers of the country through military strength. They also relied on various forms of coercion and the use of such paramilitary units as the Afghan secret police force (State Information Service, or Khadamate Ettelaate Dowlati in Dari— KhAD) and the dreaded and pervasive Soviet secret police (KGB) to help maintain the new order.

Although the Soviets justified their invasion of Afghanistan as a defensive move aimed at protecting the Soviet Union's southern provincial borders from infiltration by fanatical Islamic radicals, the USSR had actually coveted the mineral-rich country of Afghanistan for its natural resources since Tsarist times. Afghanistan's vast mineral deposits include copper, iron, lead, zinc, mercury, tin, chromium, lithium, tungsten, niobium, gold, and uranium, among others, as well as a variety of precious stones. Afghanistan also boasts large deposits of combustible hydrocarbons, including coal, lignite, peat, and oil.

To protest increasing Soviet intervention and to escape the ravages of war, several million Afghans uprooted themselves and left their homes between the invasions in 1979 and 1985, most to the safety of neighboring Pakistan and Iran. As many as one-third of Afghanistan's 15 million people are currently thought

The city of Herat, with a mosque in the center

*Refugees of war made their way
mostly to neighboring Pakistan.*

to be living outside the country, awaiting the opportunity to return. Another third were chased from their towns and villages by Soviet intervention and forced to resettle in nearby camps, towns, and cities. Many of these Afghans, as well as some of those who left the country, joined the *mujahedin* and have borne arms in a continuing effort to free their land from foreign invaders.

Mujahedin casualties have been high. But, as one *mujahed* told a *New York Times* correspondent, "We will fight the Soviet intruders until there isn't a single Afghan left to pick up arms."

It was a dramatic statement that might very well have come true except for one thing—the Afghan spirit to survive.

CHAPTER THREE
OFF TO WAR

For the resistance fighters in Afghanistan, the struggle has become the center of their lives. The experiences here described, of a *mujahed* given the name Abdul Ahad, are drawn from personal accounts, and serve to illustrate the impact of the war on the people and the strength of their commitment to the struggle.

Abdul Ahad was a tall, stout man in his late thirties. Before the Soviet takeover of his country, he had worked raising grain in his family's fields near the town of Mazār-i-Sharif just south of the Soviet border. When a Russian Mi-8 assault helicopter skirted the town, spraying a wide pattern of machine-gun fire into the huts of those believed to be sympathetic toward the *mujahedin,* three of Abdul Ahad's best friends were killed. One of them was his brother.

Abdul Ahad pulled his blanket from his shoulder, shook it free of dust and sand, and flung it around his back and up over his head to keep off the chill of the Afghan night. An Afghan's blanket is one of his most prized possessions. While most Afghan women true to their Muslim heritage wear a *chadari,* covering every part of their body except their eyes, a man uses his

Afghan women wearing the traditional garb

blanket to keep his head cool. He spreads it on the ground as a clean area for prayers. He drapes it over his back like a curtain for privacy when he has to relieve himself in an open field. He ties the ends into knots so that it becomes a sort of pack for carrying things. He folds the blanket beneath him to use as a cushion to keep his trousers from getting dirty when he sits on the ground.

Abdul had come alone to the town of Pul-i-Khumri to join forces with the *mujahedin* to fight the Soviet invaders. As long as the foreigners, or *farangi,* were in his country, Abdul and his family would never be safe.

After being shown to the quarters where he was to spend the night, a group of seasoned *mujahedin* led by a man named Mussa Khan joined them. Khan was short, stocky, with a dark complexion, darkened even further by the relentless harshness of the Afghan sun. Abdul Ahad stood quietly off to one side as the others talked of their recent journey from Pakistan, where they had tried to obtain weapons and more men to continue the war against the Soviets.

In time, a serving boy no older than fourteen brought an ewer of water and a large basin with a wide brim and a perforated cover. The boy slipped silently from man to man, pouring water over the hands of each of them, including Abdul Ahad. The men rubbed their hands together as the water trickled down into the bowl.

When the boy finished his duties, Abdul Ahad joined the others, seating himself on a long oilcloth spread on the floor. The men sat shoulder to shoulder around its perimeter, facing two small kerosene lamps burning brightly in the center. The boy returned shortly, carrying a basket of flat pieces of bread called

Children bringing tea and
bread to the mujahedin

nan and separate platters of rice and fatty meat, which were set before the men.

Abdul Ahad ate quickly, using his fingers to scoop up some rice, form it into a ball, and stuff it into his mouth. Then he tore off a piece of meat, wrapped some bread around it, and ate that, too.

As the meal continued, the serving boy brought a pitcher of water and poured some into a tall metal cup. As each man finished drinking, he put the cup on the oilcloth, where the boy refilled it for the next user. Soon the food was gone, and the dishes, scraps of bread, and oilcloth were removed. Then the boy brought water for washing the men's hands.

After the meal, a small glass was set before each man, and the boy filled the glasses with *chai*, or Afghan tea. Some of the men talked for the first time since the meal had begun; others smoked cigarettes or stuffed pinches of *naswar*, a mixture of tobacco and various strong spices, behind their lips or inside their cheeks. After a while, the men chewing *naswar* spit it into a small metal container shaped like an hourglass with an open top.

Mussa Khan called to one of the men from his group and began talking to him in a dialect that Abdul Ahad couldn't understand. Abdul watched the man's face carefully, picking up an occasional word but unable to derive any meaning from the conversation. Eventually, the man looked over to Abdul Ahad, nodded in agreement at something Mussa Khan had said, then rose to his feet and approached Abdul.

"You are Abdul Ahad of Mazār-i-Sharif, and you've come to join Mussa Khan and his *mujahedin* in their battle to free our land from the *farangi*," he said, extending his hand for Abdul to take.

"Yes," Abdul said, smiling back at the tall, lanky stranger. From his dialect, Abdul could tell he was an

Uzbeki. The man had deep-set, friendly eyes and a childlike innocence in his young-looking face, although from the size and nature of the man Abdul guessed him to be near his own age of thirty-eight.

"That's very good," the Uzbeki said. "I am Mustapha Shah. Mussa Khan and I welcome all who wish to join the battle. Have you a weapon?"

Abdul Ahad shook his head.

"You are brave to travel unarmed all the way from Mazār-i-Sharif to Pul-i-Khumri. Tomorrow we will leave for our base camp near the Pakistani border to join several others who have been fighting the invaders near Jalalabad. We will get additional arms there and return by the end of the week."

"Where will we fight first?" asked Abdul Ahad.

Mustapha shrugged. "Wherever we are needed," he said.

One by one, the men in the room spread their blankets on the floor, removed their shoes, and began to pray—standing, bending, kneeling, sitting on their heels, standing again, bending again, all the while lips moving silently with the sacred words in their minds. It was the custom for Abdul Ahad, as well, and he quickly followed suit. But when he finished, he found his heart thumping wildly. He had seen the war and felt its sting with the death of family and friends. Now he was actually going to become part of it. The thought was both glorifying and frightening. The religion of Islam guarantees that any person who dies fighting for the cause of Islam will be rewarded with a place in heaven. But the thought of dying was something Abdul could not take lightly.

Still, Abdul Ahad didn't want to go on living with fire and thunder falling from the sky onto him and his family. There was no way around it. He was a *mujahed* now, and he would fight.

Abdul watched as the boy came in once again and passed out thin, narrow mats, which the men spread out on the floor, covering nearly every inch of space. The evening chill had worked its way inside, and Abdul settled onto his mat, pulling his blanket up over his chin. In time, the last of the kerosene lamps was blown out and darkness fell over the room. Soon Abdul heard nothing but the stillness of the night, broken only by snores.

With the crowing of the cocks and the distant sound of a *muezzin* intoning the call to morning prayer, Abdul stirred. He opened his eyes slowly to the first beams of sunlight streaming through the window overlooking the narrow courtyard. Most of the men in the room had already arisen. Some were gone.

Abdul arose and washed his face, ears, arms, feet, legs, and genitals, as was the custom. Then he began his morning prayers, the first of five sets that Muslims must say every day. When he finished, he was taken by Mustapha Shah to meet Mussa Khan. Abdul was surprised to find that the *mujahedin* leader spoke excellent Pashtu. The two talked comfortably about the night's sleep and the weather for several minutes before an elderly man dressed in plain cotton pants and a shirt came up and summoned Mussa to his side.

Abdul sat cross-legged next to several other men who were eating breakfast. He was served *chai* with three cubes of sugar at the bottom of a small glass. Abdul drank the tea without stirring it, and the glass was filled again. Only some of the sugar had dissolved, with enough remaining on the bottom of the glass for

A mujahedin *in prayer*

* 50 *

several more refills. These, too, he drank as he tore off small pieces of warm *nan* and stuffed them into his mouth.

A breakfast of *nan* and tea is customary in Afghanistan, as is the manner in which the meal is consumed. If a person drinks from a shared glass, he or she must either finish it or throw its contents away before setting the glass down for the next person to use. If food is dropped on the ground, it must be picked up so that no one defiles it by stepping on it.

When Abdul was young, he was chided by his father for rolling up his pantlegs so that they wouldn't drag in the mud and get soiled. His father then taught him the traditional way of rolling the waistband under the drawstrings to raise the cuffs. Some Afghans believe that following strict customs helps keep spies from being able to infiltrate the community.

As Abdul washed the last few crumbs of bread from his hands, a loud whistling noise followed by a huge explosion shook the building. The men inside broke into a flurry of activity, each shouting directions to the next until finally Mussa Khan held his hands high and broke through the commotion with a loud, clear voice.

"The *farangi* have come," he shouted. "Grab your weapons and follow me!"

Abdul froze. Was this the beginning of his training as a soldier? And what was he to use in the battle against Soviet missiles—his small pocketknife and a handful of stones?

All at once several more explosions louder than the first rocked the building. The men grabbed their weapons and hurried out the door and down the ladder on the heels of their leader. In their hands they carried recently captured Soviet AK-47s and centuries-old single-shot carbines. In a moment, Abdul Ahad was out the door, shimmying down the ladder, through the first floor of the house, and out into the courtyard leading to a narrow alleyway. A hand reached out and grabbed him by the arm.

"Stay close to the wall, Abdul," Mustapha shouted, "or the gunships will see you!"

From the distance Abdul heard the pulsing beat of the helicopter rotors. They sounded strangely calming, almost soothing. And then the shriek of a missile grew louder with alarming speed.

Mussa Khan motioned the men through a small doorway cut into the side of a dome-shaped hut at the end of the street. As Abdul hurried inside, he banged his head against the arch overhead and was pushed down a small flight of stairs until he went sprawling to the floor. In the darkness, he could make out the silhouetted form of Mussa Khan peering out from the doorway into the morning light. Abdul's vision blurred and he felt lightheaded. He was overwhelmed by the sounds of the missiles exploding as they zeroed in on their targets, the swirling movements around him in the room, the sight of Mussa Khan swaying in the doorway, and the shoving and pushing of a roomful of men struggling to their feet.

Suddenly everything went black.

* * *

Abdul Ahad woke to the sound of men's laughter. He was lying on his back peering up into the light from a single glowing lamp. He recognized Mussa Khan, hands on his hips, standing over him.

"So, Abdul Ahad. You have experienced your first battle and sustained your first wound. How do you feel?"

Abdul was confused. He reached up to his head and flinched. Pain shot from his head down his neck and into the center of his back. When he pulled his hand back, he noticed traces of blood.

"What happened?" he asked.

Several of the men laughed as Mussa Khan held his hand out to Abdul. "You must have banged your head on the doorway," Mussa replied. "You have a head wound, your first battle scar."

Abdul took the older man's hand and was surprised at the strength that pulled him to his feet. For a moment, Abdul felt weak and thought he might pass out again. One of the others grabbed his free arm and held Abdul upright until the dizziness passed.

"The Soviet gunships," Abdul said, looking around the bare room. "Where are they? Did we fight them off?"

At that, the entire room broke into laughter.

"It's hard to fight off gunships with these," the leader said, holding out his Soviet-made Kalashnikov automatic rifle. "Come. The bombing has stopped. We will go back outside into the sunlight, where brave *mujahedin* belong."

Abdul followed the others up the stairs and out into the street. He squinted at the bright light as it flashed across his face. From the height of the sun, he estimated the time as 11 A.M., nearly four hours since the gunships had sent them scurrying for cover. As his eyes grew accustomed to the light, he was amazed to find several buildings, including the one in which he had spent the night, reduced to a mass of rubble.

Abdul Ahad felt a mixture of remorse and pride. The thought that he had come close to death frightened him. The thought that he had survived gave him courage. He wondered as he walked along the dusty roadway leading from town if his brother had felt the same mixture of fear and strength when the helicopters had come to Mazār-i-Sharif.

CHAPTER FOUR
INTO THE BATTLE

Amu Bhad poked Abdul in the ribs and laughed.
"Would you believe it? I am an educated man, a world
traveler. Before the war, I prayed with the *ayatollahs* in
Iran and with the *mullahs* in Pakistan. I spent three
months in England, studying Dari at Oxford University there. And you, Abdul Ahad, are you from
Bamian?"

Abdul shook his head. "From Mazār-i-Sharif. I
am a farmer."

Amu Bhad thought quietly for several seconds as
the two men walked along the path, an occasional peb-
ble kicking up from beneath their heels and tumbling
toward the valley below, betraying their presence.

"Mazār-i-Sharif," he echoed finally. "You are an
Uzbeki, then?"

Abdul Ahad nodded.

"But you speak Pashtu. How is it that an Uzbeki
farmer from Mazār-i-Sharif speaks Pashtu when his
brothers all speak Uzbek?"

"Mussa Khan is an Uzbeki," Abdul replied, "and
yet you hear him speak Pashtu."

"Mussa Khan is a great man," Amu said, "and very
brave. He speaks Pashtu and Uzbek and Dari as well as

anyone I have known. And several other dialects, too," he added.

Abdul shrugged. "So if a brave man can speak more than one dialect, why not a farmer?"

Amu Bhad thought for several moments before breaking into a laugh once again. "By Allah," he said, "I like a man who speaks dialects and carries his wits about him. That is the kind of *mujahedin* we need. We will be friends, Abdul Ahad, *Insha'Allah* [God willing]."

The small, wiry man with eyes like saucers held out a bony hand, which Abdul grasped. Although the man seemed friendly enough, there was something about him that made Abdul uneasy. It was true that he seemed well educated, and Abdul didn't doubt that the man had traveled both in and outside Afghanistan, as he had said. Still, something about him—perhaps it was his laugh, which was intended to put people at ease— made Abdul wary.

As the *mujahedin* walked along the barren land- scape, Abdul looked back over his shoulder. There, several yards behind, he saw Mustapha glancing back nervously, as if expecting to find someone following them. Abdul slowed his pace until Mustapha caught up to him.

"You look back often, Mustapha."

Mustapha smiled. "I am worried that a dog may be following us," he said.

It was an obvious evasion, and Abdul pressed Mustapha about it.

"On the way out of the village," Mustapha finally admitted, "there were two men who stopped to give us directions to Nahrin."

"I remember them."

"I've seen one of them before, at the University in Kabul. I think he was a communist, a Karmali."

"So?" Abdul asked. "Lots of university students in Kabul are communists."

"But he wasn't a student. He was a professor. And I saw him eyeing us in a way that made me uneasy. I think maybe he is a member of KhAD, Karmal's secret police. Otherwise, why would a professor from the university and a member of the communist party be living in a small town so far from Kabul?"

The words made Abdul's mouth turn dry. The KhAD forces were some of the most feared and hated in the country. KhAD agents worked for Babrak Karmal, the Soviet-installed leader of the puppet government in Kabul, assembling information on the movements of the *mujahedin* and passing it along to the *Shuravi*, the Soviets. The military used the information to plan their air attacks on *mujahedin* strongholds. If Mustapha were right, he and the rest of the *mujahedin* could be walking right into a Soviet trap. No wonder Mustapha was uneasy.

The group continued to the top of a mountain pass. There, a long, narrow valley opened up before them. Several thousand feet below, a snakelike thread of silver-blue marked the course of a mountain stream. At the end of the valley was another mountain range that had to be crossed to reach the town of Nahrin. It was there that Mussa Khan would barter for arms for his men so that they could continue their fight against the *Shuravi*.

An hour later, the group stopped along the stream near a collection of tents. A group of farmers tossing bright clouds of grain into the air against a backdrop of deep purple mountains were separating wheat from chaff. Mussa Khan knew several of the men, and after the customary embrace, the farmers pulled *nan* from their sacks and presented it to the *mujahedin*.

The mountains of Afghanistan have always served as its best defense. Forts perched on top of crags gave sweeping views of the roads leading into the country.

Mussa Khan asked the farmers about the war, and they replied that the *Shuravi* had bombed their village just days before and killed many people. So now they lived in camouflaged tents in the valley, their women and children hidden from the low-flying Soviet planes and helicopters.

"We, too, fight the *Shuravi*," one of the farmers told Mussa Khan. "We sell our corn, our horses, everything we own in order to buy guns and ammunition to protect our people. We wait for help from Peshawar, but it never comes. One month ago, the *Shuravi* came and took thirty people away for helping the *mujahedin*. Some say they are in prison at Konduz, but others say they were executed. No one knows for sure."

After a brief rest, Mussa Khan thanked his hosts, and the *mujahedin* set off along the stream toward Nahrin. The footing was treacherous, with large rocks and small, slippery stones that had tumbled down from the mountains on either side and settled in an uneven heap along the edge of the stream. The group was walking slowly upward toward the last range of mountains when a Pashtun in bright red cotton pants and with a black patch over his right eye pulled from his pocket a small hollowed-out gourd painted in several shades of blue and green.

The eye-patched Pashtun lifted the hinged top of the gourd and dipped his fingers into a coarse mixture of *naswar*, extracting a small wad that he stuffed between his lower gums and lips.

"Here," the man said, holding the container out for Abdul. "From an old family recipe. It is the finest, purest *naswar* in the Panjshir. Try some. It will put the spring back into your feet."

Abdul didn't often take *naswar*, but he didn't want to offend the Pashtun, so he dipped his fingers into the

Shells are distributed among the
mujahedin *at a small Afghan village.*

gourd and stuck a small wad of the tobacco-and-spice mixture beneath his tongue, where it burned like fire and curled his lips into an involuntary sneer. For a moment, he thought about spitting it out, but that would be an insult, so he gritted his teeth and tried to smile.

The Pashtun grinned confidently. "I see you recognize fine *naswar* when you taste it," he said, closing the lid on the gourd and slipping it back into his pocket. "Remember there is more when you want it."

Abdul would remember. He was certain of that.

Suddenly from behind them Abdul heard a sharp "crack!" like the distant burst of a firecracker. It was followed by another, and then another. Mussa Khan at the lead turned quickly toward the ridge on their left, his eyes scanning the rocky crags hanging high above them.

Another crack sounded, this one louder than the others, and Mussa shouted for the *mujahedin* to take cover. Abdul froze for a second, then followed as everyone stumbled toward the safety of a mass of boulders at the base of the ridge. A volley of automatic rifle fire split the still afternoon air.

Abdul dove into a gully, then leaped up and raced toward cover on the opposite side of the ridge. Mustapha crashed through some scrub poplars and pulled up beside Abdul. The steady crackle of rifle fire told them that the war had reached them once again.

From over the ridge where the gunfire was concentrated, a helicopter gunship appeared and began strafing the valley floor with machine-gun fire. A sudden squeal followed by a loud explosion shook the side of the hill behind Mussa Khan and the others. A thick column of smoke and dust rose about a hundred yards away.

"Keep low, Abdul," Mustapha warned as he pulled his semiautomatic rifle from his shoulder and slipped the safety off. Abdul huddled close to the base of a boulder while Mustapha peered out from one side. A pair of Soviet MiGs appeared, their twin white vapor trails highlighted against the blue sky, tracing the paths of two rockets. The missiles slammed into the side of the hill above Abdul and Mustapha as the first MiG pulled out of its dive and banked away. Soon the second MiG followed, sending its rockets deep into the hillside farther up the valley from the *mujahedin*.

Seconds later, a helicopter gunship hovering over the ridge rained down a storm of bullets on the *mujahedin*. Mortar shells exploded with a thumping sound, echoing through the valley and flooding the area with a thick cloud of smoke.

Suddenly a volley of Kalashnikov shots burst from the rocks across from Abdul and Mustapha as the other *mujahedin* opened fire. This volley was followed by several single rifle shots aimed skyward. Within minutes, the helicopter had vanished and the air once again grew silent.

Abdul's heart was beating wildly as Mussa Khan and the others across the way slowly appeared from their cover. Mustapha and Abdul joined them at the stream, dusted themselves off, and reloaded their weapons. One of the men, an experienced *mujahed* from the Panjshir Valley, had been shot. Two others had carried him from the hillside and were working to lash together a stretcher from blankets and rope. The wounded man had a thick black beard and bushy eyebrows. His darkened face was covered with blood. His eyes were half open, but he was unconscious.

Abdul and two others lifted the man and placed him on the blankets, which four *mujahedin* then lifted between them. With Mustapha falling back, eyes scanning the sky above and behind them, the men jogged as quickly as they could up the pass leading to Nahrin.

It was evening by the time the *mujahedin* reached their destination. At Nahrin, they met six other *mujahedin,* one of whom had a medical kit with which he tried to patch the wounded warrior. Finally the men decided to send a runner to the far end of town for a truck that would take the man to a Red Cross hospital in Jalalabad. He had lost a lot of blood. His pulse was weak. Everyone knew he would probably not survive the jolting ride over the rough mountain roads.

The *mujahedin* walked toward the safety of their night's lodging. Along the way, they were joined by a *mujahed* who had just come down from the hills. He was twenty years old, happy and laughing, and he said that the fight was over. The *Shuravi* had retreated back to Kabul, from where they'd come.

As the young man strode away, Mussa Khan turned toward his men. Tomorrow would be a new day, he told them. And there would be new battles. They would get up early to buy weapons. Then they would head back into the hills to meet the Russians.

CHAPTER FIVE
THE MIDDLE YEARS

By 1985, the war had turned into a stalemate as each side—the Soviets-Afghans and the *mujahedin*—laid claim to certain strategic areas. Through the first six years, the guerrillas succeeded in threatening the general security of many of the Soviet-held positions, including the capital city of Kabul. The *mujahedin's* attacks consisted of assassinations and kidnappings of both Soviet and Afghan regime officials, interruptions of supply convoys necessary to keep Soviet troops at full fighting strength, bombings, ground assaults, and rocket attacks.

From a distance, Kabul was the picture of business as usual. Merchants sold their wares along the banks of the Kabul River while young children played a game similar to field hockey. Just outside the secured buffer zone, though, the *mujahedin* were constantly poised and ready to strike. Kabul was a city under siege.

The rebel activities surrounding Kabul and other Soviet-held cities ebbed and flowed with the changing of the seasons. Each winter, military activity eased as the snows and bitter cold swooping down from the Hindu Kush hindered troop mobility on both sides.

But with the first warm days of spring came renewed assaults. One of the largest since the 1979 invasion occurred in Kabul in early September 1984 and resulted in a violent two-hour battle near the military base at the ancient fortress of Balar Hissar.

With a large, heavily armed force of guerrillas, the *mujahedin* launched a rocket assault that destroyed fifteen Soviet armored vehicles and killed forty to fifty Afghan soldiers. In retaliation, the Soviets launched a massive air assault on several nearby villages, killing large numbers of civilians.

As the frequency of such *mujahedin* attacks on Kabul increased, the Soviets tightened security throughout the capital city and its airport, stepping up their own attacks on nearby rebel strongholds from which the *mujahedin* were thought to be operating.

In 1984, the *mujahedin* attacked and destroyed pylons at the hydroelectric plant east of Kabul, causing severe electrical shortages in the city. Many homes were without electricity, and industrial output ground to a halt for a number of weeks.

Several groups of *mujahedin* working together continued their rocket attacks on Kabul into November. They managed to down a Soviet helicopter, resulting in the death of a high-ranking Soviet general. In retaliation, the Soviets ordered more air attacks against the villages south of the capital.

In early 1985 the *mujahedin*'s efforts resulted in the deaths of sixty Soviet troops. The Soviets responded by setting up a tightened security network of eight concentric circles around Kabul. Each post contained a hundred soldiers plus eight to ten tanks.

In the summer of 1985, *mujahedin* units again stepped up pressure on both Kabul and its airport, rocking the area with bombs, mortars, and ground-to-ground missiles. The Soviets' inability to prevent such attacks shook their confidence and led to ever-tightening security measures. More armed patrols were established in areas of high concentration of government and military personnel, and helicopters on night patrol over Kabul were fitted with special light-intensifying equipment.

While Kabul remained one of the *mujahedin's* favorite targets, the Panjshir Valley was the secondary center of their activities. Guerrilla fighters under the command of Ahmad Shah Massoud of the Jamiat-i-Islami group regularly attacked Soviet convoys passing through the valley on the highway south to Kabul. In late April 1983, the Soviets broke a truce with Massoud by launching a campaign to destroy resistance in the valley and eliminate Massoud as a leader.

For the first time since the occupation, the Soviets initiated sweeping raids in bombers launched from the Soviet Union. They committed to the campaign nearly 20,000 men supported by several thousand Afghan soldiers plus local militias. The Soviets also occupied adjacent valleys in an effort to seal off the Panjshir and prevent the escape of Massoud and his guerrillas.

The Soviet assault failed as Massoud and his *mujahedin* continued their hit-and-run tactics, inflicting heavy damage on Soviet forces before withdrawing from the valley floor to the safety of the surrounding mountainside. Although the *mujahedin* lost significant numbers during the assault, their tactical units remained in force. Meanwhile, Massoud's group estimated Soviet-Afghan army losses at 2,500 killed and wounded.

The Soviets maintained their bases in the Panjshir around Peshghor through most of 1984, launching limited sweep operations during November. Soviet

Tu-16s bombed suspected guerrilla strongholds from high range. In 1985, they carried out a major offensive in the area by bringing in a motorized rifle division of about 12,000 men and mounting bombing raids with Tu-16s and Mi-24 helicopter gunships. Massoud again escaped by withdrawing under pressure to the safety of mountain retreats.

Although the Soviets failed in their primary objective of securing the valley from *mujahedin* guerrillas, they succeeded in forcing as many as 150,000 people to flee their homes. Most of the Panjshiris took refuge in neighboring valleys, hoping to return once the Soviet military pressure eased.

Another major area of confrontation during 1984 and 1985 included the regions adjacent to Pakistan— Paktia, Paktika, Nangarhar, and Konarhā provinces on the Pakistani border. In an effort to seal the border-crossing routes between the two countries, the Soviets fortified garrisons with both Soviet and Afghan troops and conducted massive sweep operations and bombing raids in these provinces. In the process, more than forty violations of Pakistani airspace and fourteen ground incursions by Soviet-Afghan forces were made, resulting in an estimated three hundred casualties.

In the spring of 1985, after a vicious campaign climaxed by three weeks of heavy fighting, the Soviet-Afghan forces broke the eleven-month siege of Barikot in Konarha Province. Up to a hundred tanks, eighty helicopters, and sixty jet fighters were involved daily. The Soviets had hoped to seal off the border in the area by establishing military posts within the province and by paving the tortuous forty-kilometer road from Asmar to Barikot to connect the border garrisons with each other. Persistent counterattacks by the *mujahedin* eventually forced the Soviets to give up their plans.

A Soviet bomb

The fiercest fighting in any Afghan city took place in 1985 in Kandahār, where Soviet forces bombed the city daily and helicopter gunships strafed its citizens. Inside Kandahār, Soviet troops arbitrarily arrested anyone thought to be a *mujahedin* sympathizer, and shootouts between Afghan forces and *mujahedin* were common. Some 30,000 Soviet troops retained control of the airport twelve kilometers southeast of the city, while the Afghan army set up thirty military posts within the city limits. Soviet and Afghan forces also increased air attacks in an effort to drive out guerrillas.

Despite these steps, the *mujahedin* enjoyed remarkable freedom within Kandahār, coming and going nearly at will. Assassinations of various Soviet government officials were common. In reprisal for the January 1985 assassination of a PDPA official, according to a report in the French newspaper *Le Monde,* Soviet soldiers killed more than forty Afghan civilians. In return, the *mujahedin* killed thirty Soviet and Afghan soldiers the following month.

By 1985, as much as half the western city of Herat had been destroyed by bombardment, according to a U. S. State Department report. Large sections of the city were deserted, its residents having fled to nearby villages or to neighboring Iran for safety. The Soviets there were following a scorched-earth policy, randomly bombing as much of the city as possible in an attempt to eliminate all *mujahedin* hiding places.

But the Soviets did not limit their actions to the *mujahedin.* As early as 1983, numerous accounts of Soviet military action against the elderly, women, and children had been filed by the Western press. In August 1985, special correspondent for the *Christian Science Monitor* Edward Girardet reported on a massacre in the Chamar Pass region by a massive Soviet-Afghan force totaling more than 20,000.

The landscape was littered with the mutilated carcasses of animals, twisted metal pots, scorched clothing, torn saddles, and a boy's tattered slingshot, Girardet wrote. An uncounted number of victims were buried in a bomb crater covered with a tarpaulin, while battered survivors straggled off toward Pakistan.

"The Chamar Pass massacre," Girardet continued, "shows just what kind of war the Kremlin is waging in Afghanistan. By slaughtering innocent human beings, bombing farms, despoiling crops, killing animals, and wrecking fragile irrigation systems, the USSR seeks not only to punish the local population for its resistance sympathies, but also to totally disrupt the economic and social infrastructure of the guerrilla-held areas, which represent well over 80 percent of the country."

An article by Rosanne Klass, director of the Afghanistan Information Center of Freedom House, Inc., in New York, summarized a report by Rob Schultheis of the *Washington Post*, who interviewed survivors of an April 1985 atrocity by Russian troops in the Laghman Valley in eastern Afghanistan.

"In a single district," wrote Klass, "nearly 800 people were slaughtered—from pregnant women and newborns to the aged; they were shot, burned alive, hanged, bayoneted, tortured to death, killed with grenades, decapitated, beaten to death, and mutilated."

Despite such continuing atrocities, the *mujahedin* fought on. As large numbers of Soviet and Afghan troops massed in and around Herat in early 1985, the *mujahedin*, led by Ismael Khan, the guerrilla commander of the Jamiat-i-Islami group in Herat, staged a spectacular June attack on Shindand Air Base, destroying an estimated twenty Soviet-made MiG-21s. Reports from Soviet intelligence sources stated that the airplanes were blown up in such a way as to indicate sabotage rather than damage sustained from battle. One month later, the Soviets executed some twenty Afghan air force officers for their role in the raid.

Even though security at Herat remained tight, Soviet commanders decided to relocate large numbers of Soviet and Afghan aircraft from both Herat and Kandahār to Shindand Air Base. In the process, they sought increased logistical support from the Afghan army, whom the Soviet Union expected would play a more vigorous role in the war.

But it was not to be. The Afghan armed forces were trapped in inefficiency. Their ranks suffered a high desertion rate and poor morale, both of which drastically reduced combat efficiency. Despite large infusions of aid, the Soviets failed to transform the Afghan army into the viable fighting machine they had hoped it would become.

Discord within the PDPA continued to plague the Afghan army. Army officers and enlisted men with Khalq (People's Party) political ties complained bitterly about the preferential treatment given Parcham (Banner Party) soldiers by the Marxist-dominated Parcham regime in Kabul. In retribution, many Khalq party members, which included a large number of PDPA troops, secretly assisted the *mujahedin* whenever possible.

Listed in late 1978 at a strength of 110,000 men, the Afghan army actually numbered closer to 80,000. One year later, desertion and casualties had thinned the ranks to 20,000 men. That number was boosted by the draft to around 40,000 men by mid-1985, but an unusually high turnover rate of around 10,000 men annually continued to plague the force.

Although both officers and enlisted men were paid generously by Afghan standards to serve in the army, the ranks were filled with unqualified troops, including a large number of youngsters who had been unfortunate enough to be caught by the draft. There were numerous cases of men being drafted, deserting, getting caught, and being drafted again. Due to the shortage of able young men, the draft age was lowered in 1984 from seventeen to sixteen years of age. To ensure an adequate supply of soldiers, the term of service was lengthened from three to four years. These changes in the military conscription laws resulted in even more mutinies and desertions to the *mujahedin*. Those soldiers who didn't desert often worked secretly to foil army operations by allowing *mujahedin* to evade capture or defeat.

One of the means the Marxist regime in Kabul used in attempting to reduce the number of Afghan army desertions was to increase the ratio of officers to enlisted men, often to as many as six officers for every ten conscripts. The officers were charged with the dual role of watching their men as well as commanding them, although officers with strong Khalqi ties proved unreliable. Their split loyalties often led them to turn the other way when their own troops sought to desert. The *mujahedin* usually welcomed captured Afghan enlistees and deserters to their groups, especially if they brought weapons with them. Many deserters simply changed uniforms and joined the battle against their former comrades.

The weakness of its ground troops wasn't the only problem plaguing Kabul. The Afghan air force in 1985 consisted of about 7,000 men and included approximately 150 combat aircraft and a smaller number of support and transport craft. Most of these were obsolete Soviet-made planes and helicopters obtained prior to the invasion. They included fifty MiG-17 jet fight-

*Afghan children being indoctrinated and trained
in war tactics by the Soviets in Afghanistan*

ers, forty MiG-21 jet interceptors, twenty-five Su-7B ground attack fighters, and twelve Su-17 single-seat attack aircraft. There were also twenty Il-28 light bombers, fifteen An-26 short-haul transports, thirty attack helicopters of the Mi-24, Mi-4, and Mi-8 varieties, plus assorted reconnaissance and training aircraft. The Soviets hesitated to supply the air force with more sophisticated aircraft because they were afraid the pilots would defect and turn the aircraft against them.

Even bolstering the air force by 5,000 Czechoslovakian and Cuban military advisers failed to improve the quality of pilots and other Afghan air force staff. Both efficiency and reliability remained low. Most often, the Soviets assigned Afghan pilots to low-priority reconnaissance or high-risk strafing missions.

The *mujahedin,* on the other hand, were a highly motivated, extraordinarily effective group of fighting men. Although deeply divided along tribal, ethnic, regional, religious, and ideological lines, they shared an overwhelming dedication to ridding the country of the hated *Shuravi.* The rebels moved quickly from one area of the country to another, most often on foot, sometimes on horseback, occasionally in dilapidated old trucks, buses, and jeeps. They fought with homemade weapons, captured weapons, weapons passed down from one generation to the next. They purchased weapons from the black market, received them from foreign countries, stole them from under the noses of the Soviets. Despite their ragtag appearance and inferior armaments, they managed to retain control of as much as 80 percent of the countryside throughout most of the war, assassinating state and party officials and attacking regime and Soviet targets even in the heart of the capital.

Part of the reason for the *mujahedin's* success was that they were not so much an army as a people in arms. Fighting men ranged from preadolescent boys to grizzled veterans of the third British-Afghan War near the turn of the century. The total number of *mujahedin* was estimated in 1985 at 90,000, backed up by about 110,000 "reserves" who consisted of Afghans willing to pick up arms against the Soviets if called on. The actual number of active and reserve *mujahedin* may have been closer to 10 percent of the total population of 9 million at the time, or nearly 900,000 men.

By the mid-1980s, there were about ninety areas commanded by *mujahedin* leaders throughout the country. Although some of these leaders held their positions because of their status in traditional Afghan society, others gained leadership based upon their tactical prowess and bravery in action. These leaders won over large groups of followers and local popular support in the regions where they operated. The most famous of the new breed was Ahmad Shah Massoud, a Tajik who commanded forces in the Panjshir Valley and who had repeatedly rebuffed Soviet and Afghan army attempts to take control of the area.

Another trend set by the *mujahedin* was their willingness to join forces with different rebel groups in an effort to coordinate action against the enemy. Afghans are used to bearing arms; they've done so in self-defense for centuries. But they prefer to act alone or with the support of small, local tribal groups. They're just as likely to fight neighboring Afghan tribes as they are a common enemy. The new breed of *mujahedin* leaders was able to overcome old social and ethnic barriers, put aside divisive animosities, and form new alliances for a common goal.

From the beginning of the war, the resistance fighters, based near the relative safety of Peshawar, Pakistan, formed seven major groups based upon their political and religious philosophies. Although these groups didn't actually command *mujahedin* troops, they acted as unifying forces for the *mujahedin* who affiliated themselves with one or another of the groups in order to gain the funds, arms, and popular support the groups could provide.

In the areas around Kandahār and Kabul, within the provinces of Ghazni and Wardak and extending to the border regions of Pakistan, the Mahaz-i Milli Islami (National Islamic Front), led by Pir Sayed Ahmed Gailani, played the largest role. Politically, it was a conservative group whose leadership had close ties to the former Afghan royal family. Gailani's authority came from his status as a *pir*, or Sufi, Muslim leader.

In the Jalalabad, Logar, and Kandahār areas, the Jabba-i Milli Nayat-i Afghanistan (National Front for the Rescue of Afghanistan) led by Sibgatullah Mojadidi, had an organized strength of between 8,000 and 15,000 men, mostly tribal Pashtuns. Its political views were similar to those of the Mahaz-i-Milli Islami.

In Ghazni, Wardak, Badakhshan, Konarhā, Logar, and Baghlān provinces, the Harakat-e Inqelab Islami (Islamic Revolutionary Movement) led by Mohammed Nabi Mohammedi was the largest group, with membership ranging from 10,000 to 25,000 men. It, too, was mostly Pashtun and was considered the most effective of the traditionalist parties.

The largest and most powerful of the fundamental Islamic groups was the Hezb-i-Islami (Islamic Party) of Gulbuddin Hekhmatyar. In the mid-1980s, its armed members were estimated at between 20,000 and 30,000 men. Hekhmatyar, a Pashtun, was a ruthless, able leader who had ties with Shiite Muslim pro-Iranian groups. He received arms and other forms of aid from Egypt, Saudi Arabia, and China, three countries that strongly criticized Soviet intervention in Afghan affairs. His group operated primarily in Paktia, Konarha, Badakhshan, Nangarhar, and Baghlān provinces.

Because of long-standing rivalries between Hekhmatyar's group and the Jamiat-i-Islami (Islamic Society) of Burhanuddin Rabbani, relations between the two groups through the mid-1980s were strained. Rabbani was a Tajik whose following included such non-Pashtun groups as Tajiks, Uzbeks, and Turkmen. The party had its strongest following in the Dari-speaking regions of Afghanistan, including Herat, Balkh, Badakhshan, Takhar, Parwan, and Farah provinces. The Hezb-i-Islami (Islamic Party) of Yunis Khalis was a small group of between 5,000 and 7,000 armed men whose reputation for good organization and fighting effectiveness was legendary.

The Ittehad-i-Islami of Abdul Rasul Sayyaf had a small number of men but good access to arms and funds from various Arab countries with strong Muslim ties. The group was confined mostly to Sayyaf's native Paghman near Kabul.

A number of other groups also operated within the resistance. One of them, the Sazman-e Jawanan-e Musalman (Organization of Muslim Youth), was started in the late 1960s by radical students at Kabul University. The organization gained recruits through the years, not only at the university but also at various training colleges and schools throughout Kabul. Among the group's more important leaders was Ahmad Shah Massoud, a skilled military tactician and commander of the Panjshir Valley forces.

Although the seven major groups of *mujahedin* often acted independently of one another, they shared three major tactics. First, they tried to prove by large-scale sabotage that the Marxist government in Kabul was not in control of the country. Second, they reduced support of the Marxist regime by assassinations, arson, and looting. Third, they weakened the Afghan army by inciting defections and discouraging fresh recruitments.

The *mujahedin* groups' initial tactics of staging large attacks against well-fortified military targets soon proved ineffective and costly in lives. As a result, they refined their tactics, staging ambushes of convoys and enemy troop contingents, destroying bridges and electric and telephone lines, and laying mines on highways and in open areas where enemy troops and vehicles were expected to pass.

First armed almost exclusively with ancient rifles, the guerrillas soon obtained more sophisticated weapons, including British-, Chinese-, and Soviet-made mortars, antitank rockets, plastic-covered mines, and a few SAM-7 missiles. Their greatest need, however, was for portable, heat-seeking, surface-to-air missiles to blunt the superior capabilities of Soviet air attacks. Little did *mujahedin* leaders realize that by the end of 1985 this need would be filled. And the face of their war would be changed.

This man's face and the child's outfit mark them as Turkmen or Uzbeks.

CHAPTER SIX
THE WINDS OF CHANGE

As dusk rolled down out of the mountains surrounding the city of Jalalabad in September 1986, Mohammed Afzal perched precariously on one knee as he lifted a bazookalike "Stinger" to his shoulder. The Stinger, one of the most deadly ground-to-air weapons in any army's arsenal, is fitted with heat-seeking circuitry that homes in on the exhausts of overhead aircraft.

Hovering above the airport in the last remaining light of day, three Soviet Mi-24 helicopter gunships were returning from a strafing run in rural Afghanistan. Mohammed Afzal carefully aimed his weapon and fired a single missile skyward. One helicopter exploded in a fiery mass, sending a shower of glowing embers earthward.

Holding back his excitement, the Tajik *mujahed* calmly aimed and fired a second and then a third missile, and the other two helicopters burst from the sky.

The shots fired outside Jalalabad that night were heard beyond the borders of Afghanistan. In a matter of seconds, the long, grueling war had undergone a major shift in direction. The change was dramatic. After more than seven years of preparation, behind-the-scenes political maneuvering, and delicate foreign negotiations, Afghan rebels fired the first ground-to-air missile against the Soviets.

When more than 100,000 Soviet troops had moved into Afghanistan after Christmas in 1979, Soviet leaders were bursting with optimism. The Kremlin had influenced the establishment of Marxist governments in Vietnam, Cambodia, Laos, Angola, Mozambique, North Yemen, Ethiopia, Nicaragua, and Grenada. Now it was Afghanistan's turn to come into the communist fold. Who, after all, could stop the Soviets? The Soviets perceived the Afghans as a weak, backward, disorganized group of people. Certainly they would be no match for Soviet military might.

The United States was still reeling from its failure in Vietnam. The last thing the American public and their elected officials wanted was to involve America in another foreign war, this one on the very doorstep of the Soviet Union.

The Kremlin leaders believed the time was perfect for seizing control of the rugged land to the south and forcing Afghanistan into the Soviet bloc. That would secure the Soviets' southern border, provide a buffer state against possible attacks from Iran or Pakistan, and furnish the Soviets with an easy route to the Arabian Sea.

What the Soviets didn't anticipate was a revival of the American spirit in the mid-1980s. Spurred on by the reelection of Ronald Reagan as president, American foreign policy shifted to a philosophy of aiding anticommunist insurgents around the world. The Reagan Doctrine, as it was called, worried some politicians who were uneasy about the attitude of support for the rebels in Afghanistan. But this support eventually became a high priority of the Reagan administration.

President Jimmy Carter had taken the first steps in this path leading to commitment to the rebels' cause. Just weeks after the Soviets invaded Afghanistan in 1979, Zbigniew Brzezinski, President Carter's national security adviser, flew to Pakistan for talks with Pakistani President Mohammad Zia ul-Haq. President Zia agreed that the two countries should join forces in aiding the Afghan rebels. Although Pakistan and Afghanistan had squabbled over land along their mutual border for centuries, Zia feared that, should the Soviets gain a foothold in Afghanistan, his country would be defenseless against a much larger, stronger adversary. What would keep the Soviets from marching into Pakistan then?

Brzezinski followed his trip to Pakistan with a call on King Khalid of the Kingdom of Saudi Arabia to enlist the support of the Saudis. From there, he went to Peking, China, for the support of the Chinese. With the Saudis, Pakistanis, and Chinese aligned with America in its support for the *mujahedin,* perhaps the Soviet victory in Afghanistan could be held off—for a while at least.

By late 1979, the United States had committed to the Afghans $30 million in aid and weapons, mostly inferior, antiquated rifles and machine guns stockpiled from previous military skirmishes. It seemed a paltry amount to throw into a war in which the Soviets had already invested several hundred million dollars in state-of-the-art weaponry. But it was a beginning.

After Ronald Reagan's election in 1980, there were some expectations that the new administration would increase aid and perhaps even supply anti-aircraft missiles to the Afghan resistance. But despite Ronald Reagan's sympathetic view of the Afghans, domestic economic programs and deepening problems in

Central America quickly pushed to the back burner the question of whether or not to provide the Afghans with these advanced weapons.

To make matters worse, the CIA conducted a study of the ongoing war in Afghanistan and concluded that the *mujahedin*, although apparently dedicated to their cause, had virtually no chance of uprooting the Soviets from Afghan soil. The Soviets were destined to win.

The state department agreed, adding that provoking Moscow by supporting the *mujahedin* was the last thing the United States should do. After all, Reagan had campaigned on a promise of peace, not war. If the United States was ever going to sign a nuclear non-proliferation and arms reduction treaty with the Soviet Union, it had to avoid any antagonizing moves. Shipping sophisticated ground-to-air weapons to the Afghans might provoke the Soviets into withdrawing from negotiations and put increased pressure on the Afghan rebels.

In addition, military advisers in the Pentagon feared that sending high-tech weaponry to the *mujahedin* would be military suicide. Those weapons, the advisers believed, would eventually fall into enemy hands. For a time, the possibility of providing meaningful support for the *mujahedin* seemed remote, and Reagan eventually agreed that he would not push the issue.

But in 1983, Jack Wheeler, director of the California-based Freedom Research Foundation, went to Afghanistan to inspect firsthand the ravages of the war. He saw villages reduced to rubble by Soviet MiG fighters and helicopter gunships. He interviewed Afghan men, women, and children, all of whom bore the scars of war.

When Wheeler returned to the United States, he was summoned to the White House for a briefing of the president, CIA, and National Security Council officials.

"The Afghans control the ground," Wheeler advised the officials. "The Soviets control the air. Take the Soviets out of the air, and they lose."

It was a startling statement. No one had ever before stopped to consider the possibility that the Soviets might actually fail to win the war in Afghanistan.

Still, U. S. officials dragged their feet. Members of the administration were unable to agree on a unified policy of aid for Afghanistan. Despite pleas from the *mujahedin,* no American-made weapons were sent to Afghanistan. And the *mujahedin* fought on.

The following year, in 1984, CIA director William Casey met with Jack Wheeler to listen to arguments for increased arms support for Afghanistan. Three years before, Casey had ordered a study of the war and concluded that the *mujahedin* were indeed a formidable foe. Still, Casey worried that providing armed support for the Afghan rebels would present the Soviets with an excuse for escalating the war, perhaps even to the extent of invading Pakistan and overthrowing President Zia, who was considered a staunch American ally. Regardless of the zeal and dedication of the *mujahedin,* Casey and his staff felt that a Soviet victory in Afghanistan was inevitable.

One of the main reasons the Soviets were able to dominate the war in Afghanistan was the role Soviet helicopter gunships played in the war. Soviet gunships often flew commandos into unsecured Afghan villages. The Soviets would land up to two dozen commandos at a time, to attack local *mujahedin* while they were at dinner, prayer, or sleep, then depart before local resistance could form.

In other deployments, Soviet helicopters would hover over a rebel stronghold just out of range of the Afghans' antiquated firearms and use their superior firepower to pick off the resistance fighters one by one. In order to deprive the *mujahedin* of places to hide in the countryside, Soviet MiGs regularly strafed small towns and villages, leaving centuries-old communities in rubble. Half the Afghan population was left homeless, while one-third became permanent refugees.

Although President Reagan acknowledged both publicly and privately that reports of these incidents greatly touched him, his staff remained adamant. The *mujahedin* could not win. For most of Reagan's first term in office, the Afghan resistance fighters received only minimal public attention and administration support. But by 1983, one of President Reagan's chief speech writers began inserting words of support for the anticommunist Afghan guerrillas into drafts of Reagan's speeches. Reagan welcomed the opportunity to present such thoughts in presidential press conferences and messages to Congress.

By 1984, many congressional leaders, including the House of Representatives' Charles Wilson of Texas and New Hampshire Senator Gordon Humphrey, were promoting the Afghan cause. Still the Reagan administration balked at making a substantial commitment in arms to the rebels. When the U. S. Senate introduced a resolution in 1984 calling for increased aid to the Afghan resistance, President Reagan pressured Congress to get behind the bill and support it, despite objections from the state department and the CIA.

In that same year, Wilson secretly lobbied President Reagan for more action. The congressman almost singlehandedly pushed through a secret amendment adding $40 million for Afghan operations to the CIA budget. Some of the money was earmarked to provide Swiss-made Oerlikon antiaircraft cannons to the rebels. Wilson also persuaded the Pentagon to begin furnishing mules to help the *mujahedin* transport their new cannons and other equipment across the rugged mountain terrain.

The following year, the Reagan administration was set to begin escalating aid earmarked for the *mujahedin*. The president signed National Security Directive 166, which called for increased pressure on the Soviets to withdraw from Afghanistan. Though Reagan and others in Washington were eager to flex the administration's newly found muscles and arm the rebels with state-of-the-art heat-seeking Stinger missiles, the Pentagon continued to object. The military hadn't yet fully equipped *America's* troops with Stingers. Why should they send hundreds of the weapons overseas?

In addition, the Pentagon insisted that the Afghan tribesmen would never be able to master the use of such sophisticated weaponry. After all, they had failed to utilize captured Soviet SA-7 missile launchers, generally regarded as simpler to use than the Stinger. Defense Department aide Michael Pillsbury and others pointed out, however, that the Soviet SA-7s were unreliable and poorly made, which contributed to the Afghans' lack of success with them.

In June 1986, President Reagan met with *mujahedin* leaders at the White House. One member of the Afghan alliance, Mohammad Nabi Mohammadi, delivered an impassioned message to America. "We are covered in blood and ashes," he said, "and need your help."

President Reagan, in turn, spoke movingly about Afghan men, women, and children who had been mutilated by Soviet explosives. Within days, all objections to sending Stinger missiles to Afghanistan had disappeared. The stage was set. The missiles were on their way.

The *mujahedin* proved to be amazingly quick in learning how to use the first Stingers that arrived in Afghanistan. Mohammed Afzal was the first Afghan to use one in combat, and he became a deadly marksman. With the first eleven missiles he fired, Afzal downed ten Soviet aircraft. He and other *mujahedin* over the next six months destroyed an average of one Soviet helicopter or plane a day, a toll that quickly surpassed even the most pessimistic of Moscow forecasts.

Within months of their introduction into battle, the Stingers were taking their toll on Soviet troops both directly and indirectly. The deadly accuracy of the ground-to-air missiles forced the Soviets to change their air-raid tactics. Now, instead of strafing Afghan targets from point-blank low-altitude range, Soviet pilots were forced to bomb from high altitudes, beyond the reach of the Stingers. The raids became less effective and much more difficult to carry out. Soviet aircraft losses mounted quickly.

At times, Stinger missiles in the area caused the Soviets to take extraordinary precautions against them. Whenever commercial airliners arrived or departed at the Soviet-secured airport in the Afghan capital of Kabul, military-escort planes would swoop in ahead of the airliners, firing hundreds of heat-emitting decoys to thwart Stinger missile attacks. Flooding the air with heat-generating decoys made it impossible for the Stingers to differentiate one "target" from another.

Occasionally mere rumors of Stinger missiles in the hands of the *mujahedin* were enough to deter Soviet air power. French journalist Olivier Roy, visiting a remote Afghan village in 1987, found a curious absence of Soviet jets and helicopters in the skies overhead. Was the reason that the Soviets feared the rebel Stingers?

"Unfortunately, we have no Stingers," the local resistance leader told Roy. "Fortunately, I spread the word that we did," the wily Afghan added with a smile. "The planes haven't come near us since."

CHAPTER SEVEN
THE KABUL AFFAIR

The rickety four-wheel-drive jeep bounced and swayed along the snow-covered path, its engine hissing and whining like an overtired child. Every four to five minutes, the exhaust pipe let out a horrendous belch followed by a black puff of billowing smoke.

"Indigestion," Mustapha Shah quipped, "too much mutton." The Uzbeki laughed each time it happened until the joke grew as stale as the air inside the jeep. Now he sat in silence, eyes glued to the glazed-over windshield, squinting to see past the snow and ice to the spot in the road where the rendezvous was to take place. Finally, after what seemed like days, Mussa Khan motioned with his hand.

Mustapha slammed on the brakes as the vehicle bucked and lurched to an uncertain stop. The three men sat in silence for several moments before Mussa Khan motioned for Mustapha to get out. As Abdul Ahad pushed against the frozen back door, he saw Mussa pull out a pistol, a Soviet-made semiautomatic weapon, from his belt. The Uzbeki leader removed the clip, cocked the gun, then jammed the clip back up into the grip. "Let's go," he said softly.

Nearly a year had passed since the day Abdul had met Mussa Khan in Pul-i-Khumri. He had come a long way since then, traveled many tiring miles, seen too much war. But now the *Soviets* seemed to be growing tired of the struggle. The communist party daily, *Pravda,* was running stories about the war every day now, and photographs, too. The Islamic underground working out of Peshawar sent accounts of young Soviet soldiers maimed and killed or blown up or lost in action—ten thousand, twenty thousand, thirty thousand. No one knew for sure how many, but it was a lot. Too many, some Soviets reportedly were saying. And that was what the rebel forces wanted to hear.

The three men walked slowly through the snow toward the mountain. The drifts in some places were 6 or 7 feet deep. Mussa carefully picked his way across a small ridge of windblown gravel leading sharply up the hill. The wind was swirling the snow in tight, stinging circles, whipping up the powder from the ground and sending it straight up in some spots, up and around and down again upon them.

Suddenly Mussa Khan stopped.

"What is it? *Shuravi?*" Mustapha asked.

"Shhh," Mussa said, peering up into the rocks and motioning. "Your gun."

Abdul picked his way to Mussa's side.

"Shhh," Mussa said again, taking the 7-mm magnum from his companion. The *mujahed* quietly slipped the bolt back, forcing a cartridge into the chamber, then slid it forward again into firing position. Carefully, cautiously, he raised the weapon to his shoulder, squinting with his left eye through the scope. He paused, waiting, waiting . . . then *crack!* On the hillside, a muffled cry rang out before a huge ram slumped to its knees, then keeled over into a deep bank of snow.

"Karakuhl!" Abdul shouted.

"Whoo-eeey!!" Mustapha cried. "Good eating to-night, *Insha'Allah!*"

Mussa lowered the rifle from his chin and looked at it admiringly before finally passing it back to Abdul.

"Good shot, Mussa Khan," a voice rang out from behind them. The three men turned to see a small group of *mujahedin* halfway down the slope. "You still have a sharp eye," the speaker added.

"And a hearty appetite," Mussa replied as the two men strode toward each other in the snow. They grabbed, hugged, and kissed each other twice in the traditional Muslim fashion, and then laughed heartily. Mussa Khan stood a head shorter than the leader of the others, a bear of a man, 6-foot-2, 200 pounds or more, wearing the grizzled beard of a holy man, with eyes that shot like fire wherever they fell.

"Mustapha!" the bear-man said, then grabbed the wiry Uzbeki.

"It's been a long time, Ahmad Shah."

The man stopped, pushed Mustapha to one side, and motioned to Abdul. "And this little *mujahed*. He is your baby brother?"

The men laughed as Abdul's face turned red.

"If so, he is the biggest baby brother I've ever seen," Mussa Khan laughed. "This is the Uzbeki Abdul Ahad of Mazar-i-Sharif. And as good a *mujahed* as you'll find."

Ahmad Shah threw his arms around Abdul and squeezed him heartily before kissing him on both cheeks. "Then he is welcome. I am Ahmad Shah Massoud."

Abdul returned the greeting, then stepped back and stared at the man. His mouth fell open as he realized whom he'd hugged—Ahmad Massoud, the greatest leader of all the *mujahedin*. The elusive ghost of the Panjshir Valley. The man the Soviets sought to kill. The cornerstone of the Afghan resistance movement.

"Ahmad Shah Massoud," Abdul muttered, bowing, "I am honored. . . ."

* * *

The meeting went on for half an hour or longer, Ahmad Shah Massoud and Mussa Khan exchanging thoughts, laughter, strategies, hope for the future. While the two men talked, Mustapha and Abdul dipped *naswar* and swapped war stories with the other *mujahedin*. Finally, Mussa Khan returned to the group and handed Abdul a neatly folded piece of paper.

"Take good care with this," he warned. "It will see you through to Kabul and back again to the safety of your fellow *mujahedin, Insha'Allah*."

"What is it?" Abdul asked.

"No," Mussa Khan said as the younger *mujahed* began to unfold it. "Put it under your shirt and keep it there until you reach the capital. "Until then, talk to no one about this meeting, and do not mention Ahmad Shah Massoud or Mussa Khan. There are traitorous militia and KGB spies everywhere who would do anything to trap *mujahedin* leaders."

With that, Mustapha led Abdul back to the jeep for the long journey to Kabul. As they reached the vehicle, Abdul looked back a last time as the sun dipped behind the ridge high above them, casting a shadow along the snow-covered floor of the valley. High up on the hillside, he could barely make out the group of *mujahedin*, the figures of Mussa Khan and Ahmad Shah fighting their way through blowing, drifting snow toward the ram Mussa had shot earlier.

Mustapha had been only partly right. There *would* be good eating tonight, but not for Abdul and him. For them, a long night's journey lay ahead.

* * *

It was nearly nine o'clock when Mustapha and Abdul pulled into Kabul. They had encountered several road-blocks, Soviet forces at various entry points checking transit papers. When the jeep finally ground to a halt in front of a large, modern building, a man dressed in clean cotton pants and a red shirt opened the rear door and slipped into the seat behind him. The man identified himself as Saboor, and he was angry at having been kept waiting for nearly two hours in the cold Kabul night.

"Do you speak Dari?" the man asked in a thick Pashtun accent.

"A little. Not very well," Mustapha answered.

"I, too," Abdul said.

The Pashtun frowned. "I will have to go in with you to get the package. They are expecting educated men, someone fluent in Dari."

"Nobody informed me," Mustapha replied. "Thank you."

"I do not tell you for your thanks," the Pashtun snapped. "It's dangerous for me to show my face in this city. Many *Shuravi* can recognize me. If one of them happens to be inside, we'll all be in trouble."

Saboor watched two Afghan policemen walking down the street, then turned back to the *mujahedin*. "Do you have guns?"

"Only a rifle," Mustapha said apologetically.

Abdul pulled aside his coat and fingered a pistol.

"Good," Saboor told him. "Be prepared to use it."

The Pashtun swung open the door and stepped out of the jeep. Mustapha and Abdul followed him.

Saboor started briskly up the stairs leading to the doorway with Mustapha and Abdul close on his heels. At the entrance he glanced quickly from side to side, then opened the door and led the way into a large, sparse reception room. "Hello," he said in Dari to the young Afghan seated behind a desk.

"Hello," the Afghan replied. "May I help you?"

The Pashtun removed some papers from his breast pocket and handed them to the clerk. The papers explained that they were to meet the assistant secretary of cultural affairs there that evening. Abdul had the uneasy feeling that the guard standing to one side of the desk was eyeing Saboor suspiciously. Did he recognize the Pashtun? Abdul's hand slowly snaked its way inside his coat, instinctively wrapping itself around the butt of the gun, his finger pressing up against the backside of the trigger where it froze.

"Abdul!" Mustapha's voice snapped Abdul to attention. The dark-haired *mujahed* was standing beside an open door at the far end of the hall. Abdul smiled sheepishly at the young Afghan clerk and walked over to Mustapha.

"In here," Mustapha said, motioning past the door.

Abdul stepped inside and sighed. "That was close."

The Pashtun had taken out a small key with which he opened the top center drawer of the desk. He removed a thin sand-colored packet and scanned the contents quickly, then lifted the receiver off the phone. "Give me 52-138," he said in perfect Dari.

"What is it?" Abdul asked.

Mustapha hesitated, then motioned his friend

closer. "The assistant secretary is a Khalqi," he said softly. "He is dissatisfied with the way the Parchamis treat him. He has information on a *Shuravi* offensive against Massoud in the Panjshir Valley. Dates, troop strength, weapons, everything."

"In there?" Abdul asked, pointing to the envelope. Mustapha nodded.

"Hello," Saboor said into the telephone. "We are in Kabul, in your office. We have it."

The Pashtun quietly slipped the receiver back onto the hook and turned to Abdul. "What did you mean before when you said 'that was close'?"

"That *Shuravi*, the guard . . . the one behind the clerk—didn't you see the way he looked at you?"

The Pashtun shook his head.

"I think he might have suspected something."

The three men stood quietly for several moments. Suddenly, the telephone in the reception area outside the office rang.

"That's the assistant secretary with our cover story," Saboor said. He motioned toward the chairs. "Sit down and try to look relaxed. The clerk will be here any moment."

A knock sounded at the door and, just as Saboor had predicted, the clerk poked his head in.

"I'm sorry," the clerk said, "but the assistant secretary just called to say that he is tied up on business and will not be able to meet with you this evening. He asked that you return tomorrow at 10:00 A.M."

"It's our fault," the Pashtun lied. "We were late."

The clerk held the door open and the three *mujahedin* slipped past him. Abdul's heart was beating frantically as he walked by the guard and out the door. The three men hurried down the steps to the jeep. As

Mustapha opened the driver's door, Abdul noticed the same two policemen huddled outside a nearby shop. They were staring intently at the *mujahedin*.

"Let's get out of here," the Pashtun said. They slipped inside the jeep and Mustapha kicked the motor's starter once, then a second time before the engine growled to life.

"Watch out!" Abdul shouted as the two policemen started running toward the jeep. Abdul pulled the pistol out of his pocket and pointed it at one of the policemen.

"*Kerack! Kerack! Kerack!*" it cried, and one of the uniformed Afghans fell forward, a large automatic pistol in his hand.

"Hang on!" Mustapha yelled. He fed the machine a burst of fuel, and it lurched forward, slipping from side to side on the ice and snow before the oversized tires finally dug in and they raced off down the road.

"*Bulam!*" the shot from the second policeman's gun cried out, shattering the back window of the jeep.

Abdul ducked down as Mustapha cut sharply around a corner, the engine screaming and the vehicle picking up speed. The *mujahed* clung wildly to the dashboard.

"We did it!" Mustapha shouted, steering like a madman into the cold Afghan night. "We did it, thanks to Abdul Ahad! We did it, Saboor!" he cried again, peering into the mirror. Suddenly a deep frown cut across his face. "Saboor!"

Abdul turned toward the backseat. There, hunched over in a crumpled heap, lay Saboor. His eyes were open and he tried to speak, but only a thin trickle of blood fell from his lips.

"Blessed be Allah!" Abdul cried. "He's been hit!"

CHAPTER EIGHT
A NEW REGIME

Although the war in Afghanistan raged on, Soviet public support for the conflict began to wane. In an effort to rekindle confidence among the people, the Russians launched various counter-propaganda campaigns, especially in the three Soviet republics bordering Afghanistan.

To further generate support, the Soviet news media expanded their coverage of the fighting. Soviet television began carrying more stories about combat achievements, decorations for heroism in battle, and special features on Soviet troops fighting in Afghanistan. But instead of leading to Soviet support for the war, the increased coverage actually had the opposite effect.

Discontent over the conflict among former military veterans and among those who might be sent to Afghanistan increased. Soviet draft evasion grew rampant, prompting authorities to criticize those who attempted to avoid military service. Reports of payments for exemptions and noncombat assignments were common.

An open letter by an officer of the Baltic Military District, appearing in the Lithuanian newspaper *Komsomol skaya Pravda,* criticized Lithuanian youths who tried to use forged medical records to gain deferments, as well as parents of draft-age youths who sought "soft" assignments for their sons.

The Soviet *politburo* grew increasingly intolerant of Afghanistan's Babrak Karmal. Soviet dissatisfaction with Karmal had been growing since 1984. There was general agreement among the Soviets that the Karmal regime had failed to heal factional disputes within its own government. The Soviet hierarchy also felt that Karmal had failed to take advantage of Soviet military and political gains.

Moreover, Karmal's well-publicized installation by the Kremlin following Amin's assassination had turned into an international liability. The government of Pakistan, for instance, failed to recognize Karmal's right to rule and refused to negotiate an end to the war with the Karmali government.

In early April, Karmal flew back to Moscow, supposedly for medical care, then promptly dropped out of sight. Karmal was still absent from Kabul during the April 27, 1986, anniversary of the Marxist coup in Afghanistan, and his supporters began to grow concerned about his fate.

Karmal returned quietly to Kabul on May 1. The following day, as Soviet troops took up key positions throughout the city, Karmal asked to be relieved of his duties as General Secretary of the PDPA "for health reasons" and was demoted to the position of head of the Revolutionary Council. The Afghan *politburo* then confirmed the appointment of Karmal's successor, Mohammad Najibullah.

Najibullah, or Najib, as he preferred to be called, moved cautiously at first in consolidating his power. In

July, he complained openly about cadre arrogance, nepotism, corruption, embezzlement, bribery, the unwillingness of Afghan soldiers to go to the outlying provinces, and the theft of state property. To help correct the situation and to solidify his own political base, Najib blamed Karmal's supporters, ultimately ousting them and packing the central committee with Afghans loyal to himself.

The replacement of Karmal with Najib, once head of the dreaded KhAD and a former secretary of the central committee, seemed to the Soviets like a wise political move. Najib was an ambitious man who was staunchly pro-Soviet—exactly the kind of person the Kremlin wanted to see heading the Afghan government.

In reality, replacing Karmal with Najib succeeded only in solidifying opposition to Najib's party, especially among longtime Karmal supporters. Numerous conflicts between the urban Karmalis and the largely Pashtun followers of Najib erupted in Kabul and other key Afghan cities. In an effort to quell the insurrections, Najib stripped Karmal of the remainder of his political power and ordered him retired on full pension.

The actions worked for a while. But Najib's nonreligious People's Democratic Party of Afghanistan (PDPA) soon earned the wrath of Muslims throughout the country, as well as in the solidly pro-Islam neighboring countries of Pakistan and Iran. Soviet-backed raids into Pakistan during 1986 further increased that country's opposition to Najib's regime.

The Soviets' all-out effort to destroy *mujahedin* strongholds in Afghanistan near the Pakistani border led to a dramatic increase in border violations. By late November 1986, air violations numbered more than 700 (compared to 200 the year before). Artillery shellings increased to more than 150 (compared to 25 in

1985). Although many of the air violations were inadvertent overflights, some were planned raids on *mujahedin* targets just inside Pakistan. The Pakistani government reported more than a hundred civilians killed and two hundred wounded in these attacks.

In early 1987, Soviet-Afghan agents began an active campaign of subversion inside Pakistan to turn Pakistani general opinion against their government's policy of support for the *mujahedin*. Beginning with the January bombing of the Pakistani International Airlines' offices in Peshawar, subsequent terrorist acts in the area included train derailments and bombings of restaurants and several well-known hotels.

At the same time, the Soviets spent large sums of money in an attempt to recruit Pakistani tribesmen to stir up trouble inside Pakistan and to support Najib's regime against the resistance. Despite these and similar policies, the Pakistanis continued to show generous support for the Afghans.

In neighboring Iran, the government in 1986 continued its call for a speedy and unconditional withdrawal of Soviet troops from Afghanistan. Despite recently improved relations with the USSR, the Iranian news media publicized Teheran's support for the resistance during the visit to Teheran of Soviet First Deputy Foreign Minister Kornienko, the highest level Soviet visitor since the invasion.

Iranian relations with Najib's Afghan regime deteriorated further during 1986, with Soviet and DRA allegations of increased Iranian support for the *mujahedin*.

Mohammad Najibullah

Iran, like Pakistan, complained frequently of Soviet-Afghan border violations. In turn, Kabul charged Iran with causing a water shortage in the western Afghan cities of the Helmand Valley, threatening to reopen a long-standing Iranian-Afghan dispute.

In India, Prime Minister Rajiv Gandhi stressed India's interest in finding a political solution to the Afghan situation. Although India continued to call for an end to foreign intervention and interference in Afghanistan, it maintained good relations with the Kabul regime and a modest program of assistance to the DRA. In 1986, India abstained on the U.N. General Assembly resolution calling for condemnation of the USSR and the presence of foreign forces in Afghanistan.

China, on the other hand, was most adamant in accusing the Soviets of creating a major obstacle to Sino-Soviet relations through the occupation of Afghanistan. In December 1985, on the sixth anniversary of the Soviet invasion, the Chinese media noted that the invasion "sabotaged peace and stability" in the area and posed a threat to China's national security.

Throughout 1986, the Soviets under the leadership of Mikhail Gorbachev, who had gained control of the Soviet politboro after Yuri Andropov died in 1984, continued to adjust their numbers, weapons, and tactics to counter the increasing military capabilities of the *mujahedin* and to compensate for the DRA's decreasing military effectiveness. Only a few thousand underutilized Soviet troops left Afghanistan during a much-publicized "Soviet withdrawal"—far fewer than Gorbachev had promised earlier. In reality, Soviet combat forces in 1986 remained at the same strength as they had been the year before, about 118,000 troops stationed inside Afghanistan and an additional 30,000 along the Soviet-Afghan border.

Later in 1986, the Soviets revised their military tactics drastically. In the past, they had relied on large valley sweep operations using tanks and armored personnel carriers accompanying up to 10,000 troops. By mid-1986, their operations grew smaller in scale and concentrated on hitting border areas, resistance supply lines, and, whenever possible, *mujahedin* weapons' stockpiles and bases.

By the fall of 1986, the Soviets had suffered at least 3,000 casualties, bringing the total number of Soviet losses in Afghanistan since 1979 to more than 30,000, at least a third of which were deaths. In addition, the Soviets and the Afghan air force had lost a total of a thousand aircraft, mostly helicopters. As the year wore on and the *mujahedin* became more proficient with their recently acquired surface-to-air missiles like the Stinger, aircraft losses increased drastically.

In an effort to upgrade equipment and shorten the war, the Soviet Union added several new varieties of ground artillery weapons and the deadly SU-25 ground-attack fighter. Existing armored personnel carriers were replaced with newer models or tracked vehicles. Self-propelled artillery units replaced towed units in many Soviet brigades.

Despite everything, Soviet forces continued to suffer from low morale problems. Disease, particularly dysentery and hepatitis, kept as many troops out of action as did combat injuries. The theft and sale of military equipment, including fuel, weapons, medicine, and auto parts, was growing at a staggering rate. The black market had become so specialized that many items could be ordered by brand name. The Soviet soldiers running the market used the proceeds to buy liquor and drugs.

Inside the Soviet Union, years of triumphant Soviet expansionism made it nearly impossible for Kremlin leaders to imagine a defeat of the Red Army in Afghanistan. But by late 1986, Gorbachev was publicly referring to the Afghan war as "a bleeding wound." The Red Army was losing. There was no doubt about it. And the staggering costs of the war in terms of materials, men, and rubles jeopardized the ambitious program of *perestroika* (economic restructuring) that Gorbachev had engineered. By some estimates, the Soviets were investing as much as $6 billion a year in Afghanistan. As many as half the Soviet troops stationed throughout the country were said to be using narcotics, mostly opium and heroin produced from vast fields of poppies grown by Afghan peasants as a means of financing the resistance. Many of those soldiers took their drug problems back with them to the Soviet Union.

Gorbachev was clearly beginning to lose patience with a war he didn't start and didn't want. It was becoming increasingly evident that it was a war he felt he couldn't win.

CHAPTER NINE
AN END AT LAST

In late 1987, the *mujahedin* launched one of the largest and most complex offensives of the war. Long columns of Afghan rebels, armed with everything from nineteenth-century British-made Mausers to new Soviet-built Kalashnikov assault rifles, hiked up the forested ridges of Kunar Province northeast of Kabul along the Pakistan-Afghan border. On November 13, more than 10,000 *mujahedin* along a 60-mile front attacked Soviet and Afghan government troops. In the first hour of fighting, *mujahedin* straddling the ridges launched rockets from a Chinese-made BM-12 at Nawa Pass southeast of Asadabad to annihilate an Afghan army post below.

In the past, the operation would have been stunted by Soviet attack aircraft, but the *mujahedin*'s use of American-supplied Stinger antiaircraft missiles took Soviet aircraft out of the war. Said one Stinger operator, "We are not afraid of the Russian jets anymore. If they fly high enough to escape the Stingers, they are too high to hit us with their bombs."

By early 1988, Soviet-Afghan army victories were becoming scarce. Losses in men and materials—not to mention billions of dollars in rubles a year—continued to mount. The *mujahedin* had surprised nearly all of their U. S. critics by learning to use with deadly accuracy the most advanced antiaircraft and ground-to-ground missile systems.

The rebels' success in zeroing in on specific targets made the movement of Soviet supply convoys difficult. Without supplies, Soviet offensive units were forced to advance, attack, and fall back, abandoning their hard-won victories even before they had the opportunity to take military or strategic advantage of them. Red Army morale fell. A few crack Soviet troops began returning from missions without ever engaging the enemy.

The Soviets had deployed more than 165,000 troops inside Afghan boundaries and just across the Soviet-Afghan border. They planted booby-trapped toys that blew arms and legs off Afghan children, sent thousands of Afghan orphans to the Soviet Union for indoctrination in Marxist philosophy, and laid four million land mines, all in an effort to drive millions of Afghans from their homes so that the Soviets could gain control of large parts of the country.

"It was an almost genocidal operation," according to U. S. Representative Charles Wilson of Texas, "but it didn't work." Wilson was one of the main reasons for the administration's success with the Reagan Doctrine in Afghanistan. Visiting Afghan refugees in Pakistan as early as 1982, he had been impressed by the determination of the Afghan rebels to drive out the Soviets at any cost, even if they had to do it by dropping grenades down the barrels of Soviet tanks.

Wilson joined forces with the Pentagon's Fred Ikle and Pakistani President Mohammad Zia ul-Haq, both of whom believed the *mujahedin* could win. Wilson called Zia "the bravest man who ever breathed" because he had resisted enormous Soviet pressure on Pakistan to abandon support for the *mujahedin*. Zia had stood up to the Russian bear.

By early 1988, the Soviet Union had had enough. The Soviets and the Marxist regime in Kabul had been negotiating behind the scenes with U.N. representatives for a favorable resolution to the war. Gorbachev announced plans for a withdrawal of Soviet troops from Afghanistan, contingent upon a large number of preconditions. Among the conditions: All armed activities by the *mujahedin* would have to cease; foreign intervention in Afghanistan, most notably by China, Saudi Arabia, and the United States (the principal suppliers of arms and funds to the *mujahedin*), had to end; talks for the formation of a unilateral Afghan government, involving both the existing Soviet-backed regime in Kabul and the *mujahedin,* had to begin immediately; and President Zia of Pakistan had to stop allowing arms and other forms of aid to pass from that country to the rebels in Afghanistan.

It took the *mujahedin* less than forty-eight hours to respond: No deal. The rebels had gained the upper hand in Afghanistan without caving in to Russian demands. They would stick to their original plan, which called for the unconditional recall of all foreign troops from Afghan soil, even if no one else in the world, including most of the U. S. Senate and House of Representatives, believed they could prevail.

"Americans are suffering from Vietnam phobia," Zia said in a speech in 1988, referring to the stinging defeat America had suffered almost two decades earlier at the hands of the North Vietnamese, and Washington's subsequent reluctance to throw its wholehearted support behind the Afghan resistance movement. "They think the Afghans can't win."

Pakistan under President Zia had played a significant role in support of the *mujahedin's* quest for victory
in Afghanistan despite several serious threats to its own
interests in doing so. First, *mujahedin* operations in
Afghanistan brought Afghan and Soviet forces to
Pakistan's border. The Pakistani government in Islamabad was suddenly aware that the Soviet army had
become its nearest neighbor. Hot pursuit of *mujahedin*
resulted in frequent Soviet and Afghan army border
violations.

Second, KhAD agents often slipped across Pakistani lines to assassinate Afghan resistance leaders
holing up in Pakistan and to create as much friction as
possible between the separate *mujahedin* factions in
Peshawar. KhAD agents also supported several plans
by Zia's opponents to overthrow the Pakistani government.

Finally, friction between Pakistani citizens and
armed Afghan refugees in Pakistan had become intense.
Competition for scarce jobs heightened the tension.
The government in Islamabad feared that, unless a way
was found to repatriate the refugees quickly, they
would become a permanent source of problems for
Pakistan.

Luckily, Zia had developed two plans for counter-
ing these problems. First, he sought increased military
and economic aid from the United States, the Arab
states of the Persian Gulf, and China—Pakistan's
closest allies. Washington alone had committed more
than $3 billion in assistance to Pakistan between 1981
and 1986, mostly because of Pakistan's importance to
American interests in the Indian Ocean and the Persian
Gulf.

Second, Zia had begun negotiating for U.N. spon-
sorship of trilateral talks between Pakistan, Iran, and

Afghanistan as early as 1981. Although Iran had refused to join in the sessions because the *mujahedin* had not been invited to participate, the talks set the stage for later negotiations, which ultimately led to a plan for the removal of Soviet troops.

Unfortunately, just as the tides of battle were beginning to turn in favor of the *mujahedin,* President Zia, along with U. S. Ambassador to Pakistan Arnold Raphel, U. S. Military Attache, Brigadier General Herbert M. Wassom, and twenty-eight others, including top military leaders, died in a plane crash on August 17, 1988. The entire world was stunned.

Suddenly, questions about possible changes in Pakistani policy toward the *mujahedin* filled the world press. Who would take Zia's place? What would happen to the revolving-door policy that let *mujahedin* rebels and organizers launch assaults from Pakistan on Soviet-held fortifications in Afghanistan? How would the change in administrations affect the funneling of aid to rebel groups inside Afghanistan? What would happen to the millions of Afghans already taking refuge in Pakistan?

Following the first general election in Pakistan in decades, President Zia was replaced by Benazir Bhutto, the daughter of Zulfikar Ali Bhutto, the former prime minister of Pakistan from 1971 to 1977, whom Zia had executed following a coup in April 1977. President Bhutto, the first woman in history to assume leadership of a Muslim nation, proved an equally tough foe for the Soviets. There would be no major changes in Pakistan's support for the *mujahedin* in Afghanistan, she announced. The only way to end the conflict was for a complete withdrawal of Soviet troops from Afghan soil.

The Soviet Union found itself with its back to the

Pakistani President Benazir Bhutto

wall. Growing pressure by the United Nations, increasingly adverse world opinion, and spiraling problems at home forced Gorbachev to revise his list of demands. Much to the chagrin of the Marxist government in Kabul, the Soviet Union announced a schedule for complete and unilateral Soviet withdrawal from Afghanistan.

The *mujahedin* had won. The Soviets signed peace accords in April 1988, outlining a step-by-step plan for Soviet troop withdrawal from Afghanistan to culminate on February 15, 1989. According to Soviet reports, half their troops were removed by August 15, 1988, well ahead of schedule. As the withdrawal continued through 1988, the Soviets left behind an uncertain future for Moscow's southern neighbor, a tarnished image for the Kremlin's military machine, and some hard questions that remained to be answered by Mikhail Gorbachev.

The communist regime in Kabul remained in power, but political and military experts—although divided over how long the government could hold out without continuing Soviet support—agreed on one point: The *mujahedin* would eventually take Kabul; and Afghanistan, after a decade, would once again belong to the Afghans.

The bitter fighting had cost tens of thousands of lives and had forced millions of Afghans to flee their homes. In the months that followed the withdrawal, the death toll rose as the Soviet-backed regime in Kabul scrambled to survive on its own against an army of anticommunist rebels. The withdrawal, echoing the American defeat in Vietnam, represented a precarious moment for Gorbachev. The Soviet army, like its U. S. counterpart before Saigon's fall in 1975, had never before been forced from a war. For Moscow, the reper-

Soviet troops, glad to be going home, wave to the crowds in Afghanistan as they depart.

cussions, like those America had faced, would continue for years.

From Kabul, long columns of armor and personnel carriers snaked their way 200 miles north along the Kabul-Salang highway to Soviet territory. But one of the most difficult problems of all remained.

In Pakistan, relief workers prepared for the largest mass movement of refugees since 1972, when 10 million people moved into Bangladesh from India after the 1971 India-Pakistan war. Most of the Afghan refugees, while anxious to return to their homes, decided to delay their repatriation until the Najib regime in Kabul had fallen and the country was returned to autonomous Afghan control. Still, several thousand Afghans did set out on their own to be reunited with their families and friends who had remained in Afghanistan.

Meanwhile, the *mujahedin* continued their struggle. On February 8, 1989, Afghan rebels prepared for a massive attack on the city of Jalalabad, which controls vital overland routes to Pakistan. Control of Jalalabad was critical to the Kabul government's survival because the city supplies much of Kabul's fresh fruit and vegetables and is a principal site of electrical power generation for the nation's capital. Kabul was determined to retain control of the city at all costs. But the *mujahedin* had their own plans.

CHAPTER TEN
THE FINAL PLAY

It had been a stormy two weeks marred by infighting and political bickering. But finally, in late February 1989, the seven *mujahedin* factions meeting in Islamabad, Pakistan, agreed to a formula by which they would share power once Soviet-backed Najib was ousted from government.

Abdul Rasul Sayyaf, leader of the fundamentalist Islamic Union for the Liberation of Afghanistan, accepted the position of prime minister, and Sibgatullah Mojadidi, leader of the moderate Afghan National Liberation Front, agreed to be president. Five other rebel leaders also accepted cabinet assignments in the provisional government.

U. S. and Pakistani officials were impressed. They had expected the deep-seated differences between the groups to keep the *mujahedin* from reaching such an agreement so quickly, if at all. But in an internationally broadcast message, Mojadidi called on the other nations of the world to recognize the interim rebel government, which he predicted would be functioning inside Afghanistan within a month, *"Insha'Allah"*—God willing.

The *mujahedin* selected Jalalabad—just 85 miles east of Kabul—as the seat of their interim government. From there, they could run the newly formed government and prepare to attack Kabul. The only obstacle to moving the fledgling government to Jalalabad was that the eastern city was still in the hands of Najib. But *that*, the *mujahedin* reasoned, could be remedied.

Working in conjunction with Pakistani military advisers, the *mujahedin* in Islamabad decided that the quickest, most effective way to capture Jalalabad was to abandon their hit-and-run tactics and launch an all-out offensive against the city. To do so, the *mujahedin* would have to commit a major portion of their regional forces to the campaign. But the stakes were high—perhaps higher than at any other time during the ten-year war. Jalalabad provided the *mujahedin* with an opportunity to establish a legitimate, functioning provisional government that would vie with Kabul for international recognition. For Najib, Jalalabad was an opportunity to show the world that *he* ruled the country, even without the Soviet presence. Najib knew that if Jalalabad fell to a rebel attack, it was only a matter of time before the *mujahedin* would launch a similar assault against Kabul.

The battle for Jalalabad proved to be unlike any the guerrillas had fought before. On March 5, nearly 7,000 *mujahedin* attacked government defensive strongholds from the east, north, and south. With the aid of sophisticated rockets and artillery, they blasted their way through enemy lines, capturing the heavily defended government garrison at Samarkhel before setting their sights on the Jalalabad airport. By presenting a strong, concentrated front, the *mujahedin* believed they could split the city's defenses in two, sending government troops scurrying for Kabul.

But the *mujahedin* hadn't counted on the effectiveness of the Afghan air force. By concentrating their forces, the *mujahedin* had become a vulnerable target for the bombs and rockets of low-flying government jets. Although the rebels managed to take several jets out of the battle with Stinger missiles, they suffered a large number of casualties.

Another problem hampering the success of the Jalalabad campaign was the *mujahedin's* long-standing lack of unity. During the engagement at Samarkhel, one guerrilla faction attacked prematurely in order to prevent a rival group from sharing in the victory.

Still, despite their blunders, *mujahedin* forces managed by the end of March to isolate the airport and cut off the major road from Jalalabad to Kabul. They also kept open their own line of support from Pakistan, just 35 miles away. But it had become painfully obvious that a victory at Jalalabad would not be as easy as *mujahedin* leaders had thought. There would be no interim government installed in Jalalabad in March.

As the weeks wore on, the *mujahedin* settled in for a long siege. "Before, we would hit and run," according to Haji Din Mohammed, the top field commander of the Jalalabad campaign. "Now we hit and sit. It's a conventional war. It's no longer a guerrilla war."

From the commander's post atop a hill overlooking the old government strongholds, Mohammed could see the villages and bluffs that the guerrillas had taken during the last few weeks. Thick black smoke billowed from along the ridges as Afghan government jets attempted to bomb rebel positions. Everywhere the constant boom from *mujahedin* rockets and artillery pouring into Jalalabad rang out.

The rebels estimated that approximately 20,000 government troops were encamped in Jalalabad—

Mujahedin *scurry for cover among falling Soviet bombs and rockets*

The mujahedin *fire a large cannon toward
government positions in Jalalabad.*

soldiers pulled together from as far away as Herat in an effort to stop the *mujahedin* from advancing along the highway toward Kabul. Among the government troops were members of an elite militia called the Garde Khass; men from the Tsarandoi paramilitary police force attached to the ministry of the interior; and officers from KhAD, the secret police, as well as a large number of regular army units.

Mujahedin forces, on the other hand, numbered about 5,000. The military rule of thumb for attacking an entrenched enemy position calls for the attackers to outnumber the defenders by three to one.

How could the *mujahedin* hope to defeat four times as many government troops in a conventional confrontation? One way was by waging a war of attrition while advancing one step at a time on the ground—a tactic that was totally new to the rebels.

"At first it was a little difficult, but we learned," according to Haji Din Mohammed. "All of our skills in fighting we have learned from experience. So at first, if we use a new tactic or a new weapon, it is difficult for us to know what to do. But we learn, and then there is no problem."

The rebels succeeded in virtually cutting off Jalalabad from the rest of Afghanistan by grabbing control of the roads in and out of the city while for the first time establishing their own motorized supply lines. A convoy of trucks carrying food, weapons, and men from the eastern Afghan border town of Torkham streamed to within miles of Jalalabad daily.

The *mujahedin* had also gained control of the Jalalabad airport, toppling the control tower and knocking out radar installations as the guerrillas dug in on one side of the runway. The government's only link to the outside world remained sporadic helicopter service to a small park in the center of Jalalabad.

"The *mujahedin* fighting is going well," according to Mohammed, "but they are fighting a big enemy. For Najibullah, this is his life and death, his survival, his last stand. He has brought in soldiers from all over. Now we are fighting Afghan soldiers, communists, militia, everyone.

"But if they carried in all the soldiers from all of Afghanistan," Mohammed continued, "how do they give them food, how do they give them supplies, how do they give them morale? You can only bring in small things by helicopter. Now my men are five or six hundred meters from the corps headquarters."

The rebels were armed with light weapons suitable for guerrilla war, including Kalashnikov assault rifles and RPG-7 antitank rockets. In their initial assault on Jalalabad, the rebels captured heavier weapons, including a truck-mounted BM-41 multiple-rocket launcher and several tanks, including a new issue Soviet T-62.

"The pressure on Jalalabad is inexorable," said a Western diplomat in a May 4 *New York Times* article. "They're tightening the noose around it every day. They pick off one post at a time. They're slogging away. The . . . question is when it will fall."

The battle was not without its toll. In the bloodiest fighting of the ten-year war, nearly 600 *mujahedin* were killed by early May, and an even higher number of government troops were estimated as killed or wounded, including at least three Afghan army generals known to be dead.

Benazir Bhutto met in Washington in June 1989 with President George Bush and other U.S. leaders to begin discussions on the two countries' joint roles in Afghanistan. Both heads of state agreed to try to seek a political solution to the stalemated war. It was growing clear to all involved that, even with the Soviets' departure, a military victory for the *mujahedin* would be costly—if not impossible.

"Prime Minister Bhutto and I discussed ways to encourage a political solution in Afghanistan that will lead to a nonaligned, representative government willing to live in peace with its neighbors, to replace the illegitimate regime in Kabul. The United States and Pakistan will continue to explore any serious avenue toward this end," said Bush.

In the meantime, the *mujahedin* continue their battle. Although their attacks on Jalalabad have been repelled by Afghan army troops, the rebels recently launched a new campaign against Kabul, firing rockets into the capital city day and night since mid-July 1989. The rockets, Egyptian and Chinese projectiles launched from as far as 35 miles (56 km) outside city limits, have done sporadic damage, killing government and military officials as well as innocent civilians. The *mujahedin's* objective is clear: to divide and conquer. Najib has neither the political nor the military strength to continue a war on two fronts, they reason, and eventually will be forced to admit defeat and resign from power, opening the way for the provisional leaders to regain control of their country.

While the United States continues working through the United Nations to find a peaceful solution—a prospect Najib has begun to embrace—President Bush has promised to send the guerrillas more accurate 120-millimeter mortars, as well as other new arms, to help them hit the airfields so crucial to the continuing Soviet military airlift of supplies into Kabul. Soviet officials, in response, have threatened to give the Afghans top-of-the-line MiG-29 and SU-27 jets to replace aging MiG-21s and SU-17s, a prospect that doesn't particularly seem to worry *mujahedin* leaders.

"We will fight on until the last breath is gone from Najib," one rebel leader recently said. Whether Najib goes quietly, as he appears closer to be doing, or in a hail of machine-gun bullets, as many puppet leaders have done in the past, it seems certain that the only way to peace in Afghanistan is to clear Kabul of all Soviet influences and begin the difficult task of rebuilding the government from the ground up.

In the meantime, much of the country is gradually beginning to dig itself out from beneath the continuing threat of millions of land mines still dotting the Afghan countryside. Farmers are returning to their villages laden with wheat seed. Oxen are being purchased in Pakistan and driven over the mountains to their new home in an effort to replace the millions of animals destroyed during the ten-year war.

On the political front, the U.N. continues shuttling diplomats between Washington, Islamabad, Moscow, and Kabul in a valiant effort to find an end to the continuing bloodshed. It seems likely that a political solution is the country's brightest hope for continuing peace.

Like most Afghans, the *mujahedin* appear unwilling to compromise to get it. As they did during the invasion of Genghis Khan and Alexander the Great, as they did during the British-Afghan wars of nearly a century ago, they continue their battle to repel all foreign influence from their country. It's their god-given right to do so, they feel. It's their moral responsibility. It's their way of life.

And so the battles rage. But for how long?

"For as long as it takes," according to one rebel commander. *"Insha' Allah!"*

BIBLIOGRAPHY

Amnesty International Report, 1985. Amnesty International, London, 1985.

Atlas, Terry. "Refugees Await Time To Go Home in Peace," *Chicago Tribune,* May 15, 1988, Sec. 1, 8.

Barnes, Fred. "Victory in Afghanistan: The Inside Story," *Reader's Digest,* Dec. 1988, 87–93.

Barnett, Rubin R. "Toward Self-Determination in Afghanistan," *The Christian Science Monitor,* Aug. 15, 1989, 19.

Burns, John F. "An Army with Its Spirit in Disarray," *New York Times,* Feb. 7, 1989, Sec. A, 10.

Burns, John F. "Soviets Gone, Najibullah Boasts and Life in Kabul Changes Little," *New York Times,* Mar. 12, 1989, Sec. Y, 1.

Burns, John F. "20 Die as Rocket Hits a Kabul Bazaar," *New York Times,* Jul. 23, 1989, Sec. Y, 3.

Crossette, Barbara. "Afghan Rebel Tactic: Shut Airports," *New York Times,* Feb. 7, 1989, Sec. A, 6.

Crossette, Barbara. "Food Shortages Reported in Kabul," *New York Times,* Feb. 7, 1989, Sec. A, 6.

Hodson, Peregrine. *Under a Sickle Moon,* New York: Atlantic Monthly Press, 1987.

Hussain, Syed S., and Abdul H. Alvi. *Afghanistan under Soviet Occupation. Islamabad:* World Affairs, 1980.

Hyman, Anthony. *Afghanistan under Soviet Domination, 1964–83.* London: St. Martin's Press, 1984.

Jacobs, George. "Afghanistan Forces: How Many Soviets Are There?" *Jane's Defence Weekly* (London), 3, No. 23, June 22, 1985, 1228–33.

Jane's All the World's Aircraft, 1982–83. (Ed., John W. R. Taylor), London: Jane's, 1982.

Karp, Craig M. "The War in Afghanistan," *Foreign Affairs,* Summer 1986, 1026–47.

Karp, Craig M. "Afghanistan: Seven Years of Soviet Occupation," Dept. of State Bulletin, V. 87, Feb. 1987, 1.

Keller, Bill. "Soviets Evasive on Continued Afghan Bombing," *New York Times,* Feb. 7, 1989, Sec. A, 6.

Keller, Bill. "Soviet Troops Come Home Amid Army's Plastic Fanfare," *New York Times,* Feb. 7, 1989, Sec. A, 10.

Murphy, Richard. "Afghan Village Begins to Rebuild," *The Christian Science Monitor,* Aug. 3, 1989, 6.

"Russians Guarding Airport at Kabul," *New York Times,* February 7, 1989, Sec. A, 10.

Sciolino, Elaine. "Bush Asks Review of Afghan Policy," *New York Times,* February 7, 1989, Sec. A, 6.

Sciolino, Elaine. "U.S. Shapes Plan To Get Missiles from Afghans," *New York Times,* Mar. 12, 1989, Sec. Y, 10.

Sheppard, Jr., Nathaniel. "Senator Says U.S. Ready To Support Rebel Capital," *Chicago Tribune,* May 15, 1988, Sec. 1, 8.

Wayne, E. A. "U. S. Troubled by Afghan Stalemate," *The Christian Science Monitor,* June 7, 1989, 8.

Wayne, E. A. "Bhutto, Bush Will Set U.S.–Pakistan Agenda," *The Christian Science Monitor,* June 6, 1989, 1.

Weaver, Timothy. "Afghan Rebels Occupy Abandoned Towns," *Washington Post,* Nov. 8, 1988, Sec. A, 22.

Weinraub, Bernard. "Bush and Bhutto Agree on Afghan Aid," *The New York Times,* June 7, 1989, Sec. Y, 3.

INDEX